University Interviews Guide

Third Edition

Andy Gardner

and

Barbara Hamnett MBE

Copies of this publication may be obtained by contacting:
Prospects Education Resources
Tel: 01229 814840
Email: resources@prospects.co.uk
www.prospectseducationresources.co.uk

Copyright © 2013 Andy Gardner and Barbara Hamnett
First edition published 2004
Second edition published 2009

Published by
JFS School
The Mall, Kenton
Harrow HA3 9TE

JFS Editor: Helen Froggatt
BRW Editor: Kim Richardson
Cover/page designer and layout: Neil Sutton, Cambridge Design Consultants
Cover photograph: Toby Jacobs and Joel Walker

British Library Cataloguing-in-Publication data
A catalogue record for this book is available from the British Library

ISBN 978-0-9568463-1-0

Printed and bound in the UK by Ashford Colour Press Ltd

Contents

Foreword

In the JFS sixth form it is standard policy for every student to experience a preparatory interview with a senior member of staff before their UCAS Apply is completed and their reference written. The aim is to help students secure places on their chosen courses, to ensure that their personal statements are a reflection of their choice of course and to begin to prepare them, where appropriate, for university interviews. The interviewer will not normally know the student well and may be able to offer new reflections not only on the UCAS Apply itself, but on commitment, personal qualities and general guidance. Further advice, guidance and preparation is given by subject specialists together with the higher education team.

For more than thirty years sixth-formers have been asked to complete feedback forms when they have returned from interviews at universities. These have provided a rich resource, even an essential companion, for subsequent students to tap into for help with both personal statements and interviews. The collection of feedback forms has provided the basis for this book and we are very grateful to the generations of JFS students whose contributions have made this publication possible. We have attempted to represent any significant shifts in questions and interview practice over time. This book is based on the English A level system. Nonetheless, Scottish Higher, IB, Pre-U and students from other backgrounds, will find it useful.

Barbara Hamnett MBE
Formerly Principal Deputy Headteacher, JFS School

Andy Gardner
Independent Careers Advisor

Acknowledgements

Special thanks to **Tim Miller** and **Jackie Silverstone**.

Our thanks are due to every JFS and La Swap (Sixth Form Consortium) sixth-former who filled out a feedback form or sent us an email and thereby contributed to the source material for this book. It would not have been possible without them. Mary Nithiy, Nick Calogirou, Alex Dawes, Steve Newark, Andy Holmes, Toby Jacobs, Alka Mamtora, Lyn Dantas, Hannah Simon at JFS; Mike Nicholson, University of Oxford; Richard Partington and Jonathan Padley of Churchill College, University of Cambridge; Micki Regan of St George's University of London; Paul Teulon of King's College London; Pamela Toussaint of Southampton Solent University; Harriet Nerva, Nina Jacobs, Anna Ehrlich, Rachel Elf, Molly Sharpe and Helen Froggatt. JFS also acknowledges the support of the Leading Edge Partnership in the production of this book.

Introduction: Why and how to use this guide

Students

You may be asking yourself, 'What is the point of this book?' The commonly held belief, it seems, is that universities do not interview applicants any more. We would like to disagree with this view. While we accept that interviews are a very labour-intensive method of selection, and we can see that universities may be looking at ways to reduce the number of applicants that they interview, interviews are still happening in large numbers and applicants should be prepared for them. In fact, in the case of degree courses that train for a specific career, applicants are still highly likely to be interviewed. And some universities still interview *all* applicants who make it past the initial selection process.

In any case, even if your university application results in no interviews at all, preparing yourself as if for an interview can be extremely helpful and will be useful in preparing your personal statement. Looking at the sample interview questions in this guide, both general and subject-specific, will improve your self-awareness and give you much more of an idea about whether the course you have chosen is really the one for you.

The guide is split into two parts. Part 1 covers the general aspects of preparing for interviews and is broken into six sections as follows:

▸ **1 'Why have you applied for this course?'** This is the question you are most likely to be asked in any interview. But would you know how to answer it in a logical way? We believe that to know where you are going you need to know where you have been! This section of the book will help you retrace your steps through the thought processes that led to your choice. Once you are clear about how you came to your decision, you should be able to answer this question.

▸ **2 'Tell me more about yourself'** This section contains a list of questions you could be asked in an interview, whatever subject you apply for. They have not been made up! In fact, they are all questions that have been asked in interviews attended by students from the JFS and La Swap Sixth Form Centres in London in recent years. Do, also, look at the students' comments about their interview experiences: they are often enlightening.

▸ **3 'Is there anything you'd like to ask?'** You will find here some general tips about how to deal with this question, but the most important thing is to make sure you ask a question that you really do want to ask, rather than just going through the motions.

▸ **4 Personal preparation and presentation**. This section offers very general advice about what to expect, how to prepare yourself and how to make a good impression. If you are applying after a gap year, make sure that you have re-captured some of your academic work such as texts studied for A level or solving mathematical problems. It is easy to forget.

▸ **5 Applying for medicine**. This chapter covers three areas: GWIST – a careers education framework for those applying to Medicine, a rough guide to entry criteria for UK undergraduate medical degrees, and sample interview questions.

▸ **6 A realistic application for Oxbridge**. This is aimed at teachers and higher education advisors who want to give their brightest students a chance to shine in interviews for Oxford and Cambridge using the GRIST framework.

Part 2 of the guide is an A–Z of university subjects, with information and advice about what to expect in an interview for each subject. Remember that interviewers will be trying to discover:

▸ how much you already know about the subject you have chosen;

▸ whether you have the aptitude and thinking skills to learn more;

▸ whether you have thought about what the degree course will involve.

Information under each subject covers the following areas:

▸ **Essential and (possibly) useful A levels** (including AGCEs). We still come across sixth-formers with misconceptions about what qualifications they need to do certain courses. If you are applying to competitive courses in high demand/Russell Group universities, we recommend that you look at the 'Informed Choices' document available at **www.russellgroup.ac.uk/informed-choices** and watch the film available to view on the site.

▸ **Your chance of being interviewed**. No authoritative surveys have been carried out on this. The opinions here are those of the authors.

▸ **What you need to know**. Some essential pointers – ignore them at your peril!

▸ **Sample interview questions and students' comments**. Again, these are drawn from the interview experiences of, largely, JFS and La Swap sixth-formers.

We accept that we have not been able to include every one of the many degree courses available. We hope you will look at the entries for related subjects in order to get an idea of what an interview in your own subject may be like. The number of questions is largely a reflection of the number of interviews.

Finally, please note that we have given you the questions here, but we have most definitely not tried to give you the answers. This is deliberate! The answers are for you to decide.

Future Trends

Interviews

What is clear is that many courses still routinely interview. These are: Medicine, Dentistry, Veterinary Science, Primary Education and Social Work. In addition, many of the courses in what are broadly called 'health-related' fields, interview according to requirements laid down by the NHS. These include: Nursing and Midwifery, Physiotherapy, Speech Therapy, Occupational Therapy, Radiography, Ophthalmology/Optometry, Nutrition and Dietetics to name the main ones. Drama/Theatre Studies courses routinely use a range of selection techniques that may loosely be called interviews but that vary enormously. Some last one or even two days and involve practical tasks and performance.

Our recent research found that there are many other courses where interviews (outside the routine interviews at Oxford and Cambridge) are frequent, although practice varies across the range of universities. Most commonly, these are: Actuarial Studies, Anthropology, Archaeology, Architecture, Astronomy, Chemistry, Computer Science, Creative Writing, Engineering, English, Fine Art/History of Art, Landscape Design/Architecture, Mathematics, Music and Law, Natural Sciences, Pharmacy, Physics, Planning.

Some interviews e.g. Medicine and Law, are seeking to select students from a highly able field of candidates; others are seeking to ensure that the level of a particular skill is sufficient to follow the course e.g. Mathematics and Actuarial studies. Some courses use the interview more as part of a recruitment strategy. We have found that some Engineering and Biomedical courses may come into this group, especially where they are new courses that have yet to establish a reputation.

Outside of these subjects, interviews may take place for any subject where a candidate has, for example, had a long break from formal education or has atypical qualifications. In these cases the student may also be required to undertake an entrance examination of some kind.

Tests

The obvious tests carried out are those for Medicine, Dentistry and Veterinary Science and involve sitting the UKCAT or BMAT tests of which there is more elsewhere in this book. However, we are witnessing a significant change to the format of interviews for these subjects. In addition to the UCAS Apply form, there will be a cut-off UKCAT/BMAT score (which may vary from year to year so consult the relevant websites) after which candidates may be selected for interview. Some universities still use 'panel interviews' where a candidate will be interviewed by a panel of at least two and sometimes more people and that will include some clinical staff plus often a current student on the course and a lay person. Increasingly, institutions are using MMIs (Multiple, Mini Interviews). Although these vary, they have the same principle and format. Candidates are interviewed/undertake a task at a number of 'stations' around which they rotate. For example, this may involve, say, five stations with five minutes at each and may include a scientific task, such as examining some clinical data and drawing conclusions, to ethical dilemmas and questions related to work experience. These activities are then scored by the assessors at each station and these scores feature highly in the final selections made regarding the award of offers. Candidates are frequently asked to sign a confidentiality clause not to discuss the tasks with anyone. Although these may seem daunting, especially if candidates experience several of these, institutions tell us that the feedback from those interviewed suggests that they feel they have an opportunity to shine across the different criteria. We have found also that in Dentistry, a manual, dexterity test is not infrequent.

In the other routinely interviewed subjects e.g. Nursing and Midwifery and Primary Education, numeracy and literacy tests undertaken on the day feature along with group activities and discussions.

Other subjects are less predictable in their format and reflect the demand for courses. So, English may have written assessments and interviews whereas Engineering may have informal discussions preceded by a mathematics test.

Overall, universities are seeking to reduce the drain on resources that interviews create. It is far less common for interviews to take place in the broad range of arts and social science courses and this is reflected in the number of questions under each subject. Some well-known Russell Group institutions are applying a centralised selection model where the Registry makes the bulk of the offers using the UCAS Apply form and a formal standard offer. Only the more unusual candidates are passed through to the relevant subject departments. However, in the new higher fees climate, institutions are only too aware of the need to maintain their reputations and pay considerable attention to feedback from candidates as well as the annual National Student Survey undertaken by current students on courses. All universities clearly review their policies and practice on an annual basis.

Demographic Changes

Over the next few years there will be a decline in the number of 18 year olds. Most universities do not feel that this will affect their student numbers, although we may see courses merging and even institutions merging. The introduction of the 'ABB' rule – the ability to take unlimited numbers of students who achieve ABB in their A levels in 2013 allowing institutions to take additional students above their allocated numbers may allow some to expand considerably in some subjects. The future for current and immediate future cohorts looks promising.

Interviews: Some issues for parents and applicants

Selective interview or marketing interview

Some interviews are selective while some are more about marketing the course. If the interview is for a highly selective course, for example Primary Education, then this should be taken extremely seriously, following the advice given in the relevant section of this book.

It may well be that you are invited for interview but the reality is that the course is probably going to make you an offer. The interview is the institution's opportunity to market a course to an applicant it would like to have.

A clue on how selective the course you are applying for is can be found at **www.university.which.co.uk**; once you have found your course, look for 'percentage of applicants receiving offers'. If this statistic is 15% then you know it is very selective and the interview could be very important. If the statistic is more than 75% for example, then the interview may well be a marketing interview, provided you meet all the other entry criteria. However, even if you are likely to be accepted you should still treat the interview with respect and answer the questions to the best of your ability. If you created a favourable impression, and the course kept notes when you had an interview, this might help if you dip a grade when your results come out.

What help will they get from their sixth form?

If you are now realising that your son or daughter is applying for something that is extremely competitive, it is a legitimate question to ask their sixth form on their systems for preparation. You might be pleasantly surprised! For example they may be working with a local university/specialist teachers or careers advisors to provide this help. If you feel that there is a divergence between what we are suggesting and what is on offer then it might be worth a conversation with the sixth form team. It could be that it has genuinely not occurred to them to offer mock interviews.

Things you could pay money for

Some organisations will charge for mock interview services. It is not our place to endorse any paid-for services. The reality is that some schools (including some in the state sector!) use these services because the benefits in terms of less pressure on overworked staff can sometimes outweigh the costs. If you are getting adequate help from the school in mock interviews and test preparation, then we would argue that there may not be much point in doubling up.

Part 1

General aspects

1 ▶ 'Why have you applied for this course?'

The question that crops up in interviews time after time is simply this: 'Why have you applied for *this* course at *this* university?' It is therefore essential to have your reasons clear in your mind (an answer such as, 'I think it will be interesting, fun, exciting, etc.' is really not adequate). If you are completely sure about your reasons for applying, you will be much better equipped to respond confidently to an interviewer who will be looking to discover your motivations and commitment to the course.

The best way to clarify your ideas is to go back over the thought processes that led to your decision in the first place. So, think back.

Choosing your subject

Initially, you probably asked yourself the following questions:

▶ 'Am I interested in continuing to study something that I enjoyed at A level (or through another equivalent sixth form qualification)?'

▶ 'Do I want to do something that leads to a certain career?'

▶ 'Do I want to study something new that I feel I might be very interested in?'

Look at the following two examples. Do either of them reflect your own decision-making? The first is simple and straightforward. The second is more complex, and probably closer to reality.

Example 1

'I'm enjoying and doing very well in my Maths A level. I don't have a definite career idea yet and I'm not interested in studying anything new. I have looked at related degrees such as Economics, Computing and Management Studies but I feel that I would like to take the maths to a higher level at university.'

Example 2

'I am doing Politics A level along with English and History. My strengths are very much in the essay-based subjects. I am thinking about studying Politics with Philosophy and I may want to become a solicitor.'

The second example encompasses all three of your initial questions: You would be carrying on with Politics; you would be able to enter your chosen career after doing a GDL (Graduate Diploma in Law) conversion course; and you are picking up a new subject that you think will interest you. It is probable that you had originally considered doing a law degree but you realised that, for law, the actual university you go to is very important and you felt it would be easier to get on to a Politics and Philosophy course than a law course.

Now let us look at each of the initial questions in turn and consider some of the additional factors that should have influenced your decision.

If you have chosen a subject based on your A level/AGCE subjects, did you consider the following?

▸ Even if you do a degree that is a continuation of one of your A levels, there are still going to be marked differences in content. For example: An Economics degree will involve far more statistics and mathematics than the A level; a Biology degree will include far more chemistry than the A level (hence the common requirement for Chemistry A level).

▸ Some arts subjects, such as English, are incredibly competitive – the standard offer from most traditional universities would be A*AA–AAB. Did you consider whether you could get what you wanted from a degree by studying some other subject (for example, Modern Languages, Philosophy, Cultural Studies, American Studies, Modern or European Studies)?

▸ Science degrees in subjects related to A levels (Chemistry, Physics, Biology, Maths) are much more flexible in their entry requirements, especially at the clearing stage.

▸ Even if you do not know what career you would like to go into, and you have therefore chosen a subject you have enjoyed at A level, did you still think about the career implications?

If you have chosen a subject based on your ideas about your future career, did you consider the following?

▸ A large number of careers now have graduate-only entry – either officially or unofficially. Teaching, professional Surveying, professional Engineering, Chartered Accountancy, Medicine, Nursing and Physiotherapy are some examples.

▸ Some careers require a specific degree (for example, Pharmacy and Hotel Management) while others just require a degree (for example, Chartered Accountancy, Retail Management). It is worth noting that, for some careers, such as Law and Chartered Accountancy, employers can be very concerned about your original A level results as well as your degree results.

▸ If you choose a degree that is career specific then it must match your own personal profile. Does it reflect your interests? Does it suit your abilities? Does it accord with your values and attitudes? The way to find out is to do some research: If possible get some work experience; talk to people who work in the career area; look at information in careers libraries and on the Internet.

▸ What if you change your mind? How easy will it be to gain entry to another career field? This will vary from one vocational degree to another, but very often core skills gained in one degree can be useful for another career area. For example, a Primary Teaching graduate will have acquired very useful communication skills that can be applied to other areas of work.

If you have chosen a subject based on developing an interest in something new, did you consider the following?

▸ New subjects can be divided into two categories: degrees with a career link and degrees with no obvious career link. Which is yours?

▸ Examples of degrees *without* an obvious career link include Anthropology, Philosophy and Classics. Students choosing such subjects are prompted by their personal interests, but they also need to read up about their subject and research courses through university prospectuses. People, particularly parents, often worry about the employment prospects of these graduates; in fact, their levels of employment tend to be the same as for other non-vocational graduates.

- Examples of degrees *with* a career link include Psychology (although only a minority of these graduates become professional Psychologists) and Media Studies (although such graduates are in no way guaranteed entry into the media). Other obvious career links are Law and Accounting. Remember that the main reason to study these subjects is that you are very interested in the content of the course – what may follow on from them in terms of a career is a bonus!

Choosing a university

Let us now presume that your decision about what to study has been made. How did you then narrow down your choices to the five that you put in UCAS Apply? Your main considerations would probably have been: course content, your predicted grades, the location of the university, the reputation of the university.

Course content

- Many degrees will be very similar to one another, either because they have to meet the requirements of professional bodies (for example, Law, Medicine, Psychology and Electrical Engineering) or because past practice has led to degrees in certain fields having similar content (Business Studies is one of these).

- If course content was fairly similar, did you look into the methods of assessment (exams, assessments and modules) as a means of narrowing down your choices? Different methods of assessment suit different people.

- On the other hand, some degrees with the same title vary greatly in content (Geography, History, Media Studies and Languages are examples). Did you look closely at the course information to see what you would be getting?

- Some courses provide great variety through the range of options on offer. Some universities have an in-built system for giving you a wide range of choice (for example, through faculties). Did this influence your decision?

Predicted grades

- These will have been based on a number of things including your GCSE results and your overall performance in the sixth form. Currently the Secretary of State for Education is in the process of changing the AS and A level format. At the time of going to press, this was still in the consultation phase. Schools and sixth form colleges are very experienced at predicting the right grades for students, so you have to trust them. If schools get it wrong, it is normally because they have made the predictions too high.

- The more popular the degree course you apply for, the higher your predicted grades need to be. For example, English and Law (at selected universities) will normally require A*AA–AAB, while Medicine and Veterinary Science will want A*AA–AAA. If you are not predicted these grades then your application will probably be unsuccessful. Were you realistic when you chose your course?

- Some degree courses, such as Chemistry or Mechanical Engineering, may be more flexible. Information on the grades of actual students on courses can be found at WHICH? University (**www.university.which.co.uk**) and bestcourse4me.com (**www.bestcourse4me.com**).

Location of the university

All kinds of issues come into play here and it really boils down to personal preference. So how did you decide where you wanted to go?

▸ Did you think you would prefer a greenfield site, a redbrick university or city campus?
▸ Would you like to go away or be a home student?
▸ Were you influenced by religious or family issues?
▸ Was the nearness to or distance from home a deciding factor?
▸ What about the costs of being a student in a particular city?
▸ Does the university provide accommodation or do you have to find it yourself?
▸ Is there a good ratio of male students to female students?
▸ Are you a supporter of the city's football team?

Reputation of the university

Superb information is now available through **www.unistats.com**, **WHICH? University** (**www.university.which.co.uk**), and **bestcourse4me.com** (**www.bestcourse4me.com**) websites, including student satisfaction ratings, the annual entry qualifications that students have for individual courses and graduate employment destinations.

Finally, have you thought carefully about your reasons for wanting to go to university? Sometimes people use university as a means of leaving home, or of delaying going into full-time work. This is fine up to a point. However, we would suggest that for anyone contemplating a university course at least one of the following points must apply:

▸ You know your academic strengths (confirmed by exam results or teachers' opinions) and you would like to continue studying a particular subject at university.
▸ You have a career idea that matches your interests, abilities, values and attitudes.
▸ You have developed an interest in a new subject that matches your interests, abilities, values and attitudes.

So now let us ask the question again: Why have you applied for your course? Hopefully, you have an answer.

2 ▶ 'Tell me more about yourself'

As well as questions specifically related to your chosen course, interviewers are highly likely to throw in some more general topics for discussion. In doing so, they are trying to discover more about your personality, your values, your outlook on life and your motivation for doing the course. Here is a list of examples, with some hints from us about how to formulate your answers. Remember: You could be asked some or none of these questions. Sometimes you may have a post-offer group interview. Many interviews use objects, photos or pictures as discussion points. Some use short tests beforehand or ask you to bring or send in school work.

At the end of this section you will find some very perceptive comments given by real-life sixth-formers soon after their university interviews. Their advice is worth reading.

Sample interview questions

- ▶ Tell us about your school subjects.
- ▶ What grades do you expect to get?
- ▶ What is your strongest subject?

- ■ Make sure you are positive in your answers. If you have found a subject or topic difficult, what steps have you taken to overcome this?

- ▶ Why have you applied to this university?

- ■ This is your chance to show that you have read the prospectus, looked at the website and visited on the university open day.

- ▶ Why have you applied for a deferred entry?
- ▶ What plans have you got for your year off?
- ▶ If you have had a year off, what did you do and what did you learn from it?

- ■ Most admissions tutors will be happy with any gap-year plans, as long as you know what you are going to do, where you are going to do it, when you are going to do it, why you are doing it and who you are doing it with.

- ▶ What do you do in your spare time?
- ▶ How do you relax?
- ▶ How do you organise yourself?
- ▶ What books do you read?
- ▶ What are your musical interests?
- ▶ What sports do you like?
- ▶ What is the outside interest you would most like to pursue at university?

- ■ Please make sure that you re-read your personal statement thoroughly, reminding yourself of any points that you might be questioned on. Some interviews start from information you have put in your personal statement. Others ignore them completely. Be prepared!

▸ How did you become a senior prefect at school and what does it entail?

▸ How did you get to be assistant editor of your school magazine?

▸ What did you do for your Duke of Edinburgh's Award/Young Enterprise programme? What did you learn from the experience?

▸ Tell us about your work experience/part-time job. What did you learn from this?

■ Think about how these questions can be related to the course you are applying for.

▸ What have you got to offer this course?

▸ Why do you think we should accept you?

▸ If I made you an offer of A*AA, would you be depressed or would you think, 'Go for it!'?

▸ If you were a teacher describing yourself, what would you say?

▸ What are your qualities and what are your 'bad' points?

▸ If you have a problem, how do you cope with it?

■ Admissions tutors are now fed up with people saying things like, 'I'm enthusiastic, I can work in a team, I have good communication skills,' without any real evidence. Think of examples and evidence (maybe from a part-time job). Otherwise these statements are meaningless.

▸ Are you ambitious?

▸ What are your main ambitions?

▸ What are your career aims?

▸ What challenges are you looking for?

▸ Do you have any heroes?

■ These questions are intended to discover whether you know where you are going in life and how you are going to get there. Someone who is hopeful about the future will always impress.

▸ What do you think about student loans and student finance generally?

▸ Will you be living in halls or at home?

■ Be honest, but try to see all sides of the issue.

Students' comments

▸ 'The man who showed us round the department turned out to be the interviewer, so you have to be conscious of making a good impression *all* the time.'

▸ 'Make sure you can justify/defend *everything* you put in UCAS Apply.'

▸ 'It's important to be properly prepared. I made a list of all the possible questions I would be asked and how to answer them. I also made a list of all the questions I could ask about the course – number of teachers, types of projects, etc.'

▸ 'I had developed some outline answers in my mind, which were very useful, but I'm glad I didn't go into the interview room with a set of stock memorised answers to a set of stock questions. I was asked questions I wasn't quite expecting and I was asked questions from a different angle to how I was expecting.'

▸ 'My interviews might have gone badly if I hadn't prepared some questions of my own to ask, as the very first thing they asked me was, "Have you got any questions?"'

▸ 'It's good to know a bit about the college/university and course beforehand. For example, I was asked a question about social anthropology, which I was prepared for because I knew it was the tutor's research area (you can look in the course prospectus or at the relevant university or college website).'

▸ 'After having had five Cambridge interviews I can quite confidently say that they are not as daunting as you might expect.'

▸ 'The interview was more of a conversation than an interrogation.'

▸ 'I arrived slightly late due to transport problems but they didn't seem to mind. It did, however, put me ill at ease and I was somewhat disorientated as I was called for interview as soon as I arrived. This should be avoided at all costs!'

▸ 'There was a 20 minute group interview during a half-day open day with a friendly and opinionated interviewer. It was hinted throughout we would get offers. Very few people get individual interviews (for this course) and we were told the interviewed candidates were seen because they weren't of such a high calibre.'

What these comments tell you is to be prepared for everything!

3 ▸ 'Is there anything you'd like to ask?'

At some point in the interview you will probably be asked if you have any questions. Sometimes this will come at the end of the interview. Some interviewers, however, will make it an integral part of the conversation and the question may come quite early on. The important thing is not to ask a question just for the sake of it. Only ask something you really want to know the answer to.

You will probably have questions about the content and structure of the course (read the prospectus carefully). If these have not already been covered during the interview, then ask.

In addition, here are some ideas for you to think about. Information about the following areas is not always included in prospectuses or departmental brochures and so may form a basis for your questions.

▸ The career prospects for graduates.

▸ The opportunities for post-graduate research.

▸ The study facilities. (Is the course taught on a single site? Is there a departmental library?)

▸ The way the course is taught and assessed across the length of the course. (Are there lectures, seminars or tutorials and what size are the groups?)

▸ The personal support for students. (Is there a personal tutor system?)

▸ The placements for sandwich courses. (How are they organised? Who is responsible for finding the placement?)

▸ The accommodation situation.

▸ The possibility of meeting some students currently on the course.

4 ▸ Personal preparation and presentation

Points to remember

▸ The fact that you have been invited for an interview means that the university is interested in you, so that is half your battle won.

▸ In any interview, as in any conversation, there should be a two-way interaction. Make sure you participate and contribute.

▸ An interview can last anything between ten minutes and an hour.

▸ Interviews are usually conducted by one interviewer, but there could be two, three or even four of them.

▸ There is no such thing as the perfect interview.

Preparation

▸ Read carefully any material that is sent to you before the interview, so that you know what to expect when you get there.

▸ Re-read the university prospectus and details about the course.

▸ Photocopy or print off your personal statement and re-read this thoroughly before the interview.

▸ Prepare some questions you may want to ask (see previous chapter). Make sure they have not already been answered in information you have been sent by the university.

▸ Plan your journey. If an overnight stay is involved, plan for this as well. Do not be late or in a rush.

Presentation

▸ If you are applying for a vocational degree (for example, medicine or hotel management) it is usually best to err on the side of convention and dress smartly and appropriately.

▸ For most degrees, dress in clothing that you feel comfortable with, and that will not distract the interviewer from the points you want to make.

▸ Do not chew gum – whatever course you are applying for!

▸ Think about what your body language is conveying. Do not sit slumped in your seat wearing a baseball cap! It is important to engage with the interviewer from the start.

▸ When it comes to handshakes, sitting down, starting to talk, and so on, take your lead from the interviewer.

▸ Work on making eye contact, regulating your voice levels and putting across an appropriate level of friendliness and warmth.

5 ▸ Applying for Medicine

"The process should be approached like a military operation, requiring strategy and planning and of course a large dose of your precious sixth form time."

So wrote Harriet Nerva, the author of the medicine chapter in the second edition of the *University Interviews Guide* when she was entering medical school in 2008. Unfortunately for applicants and their advisors, things have become even more complicated!

This chapter attempts to cover three things:

GWIST – A careers education framework for those applying to medicine:

▸ **Grades** – GCSE/AS/A level;

▸ **Work experience** – What type of experience;

▸ **Interview** – How to prepare/What type – panel or MMI;

▸ **Subject** – Proving your interest in the subject through the personal statement/Does your referee think you are suitable for the subject/Understanding how the subject is studied – integrated, PBL or traditional;

▸ **Test** – BMAT/UKCAT or no test.

A rough guide to entry criteria for UK undergraduate medical degrees

We make no claims for 100% accuracy, but we attempt to give you (teachers, advisors, applicants and parents) an idea of the idiosyncrasies of UK undergraduate medical school application that you need to know about before you make a maximum of four choices. The information gathered is based on the GWIST framework, which in our experience reflects the main criteria by which the applicant is accepted or rejected.

> Do not use this information as a final reference source! Always check current online prospectuses as the information here could be out of date very quickly. This chapter is designed to help applicants make realistic applications and have a true idea of all the criteria that they need to meet.

Sample interview questions

Questions that have been asked in real interviews that can be used in mock interviews.

It should be noted that this whole chapter reflects these points from the Medical Schools Council (MSC):

1   Selection for Medical School implies selection for the medical profession.
2   The aim is to select those with the greatest aptitude for medical training from those with high academic ability.
3   The practice of medicine requires the highest standards of professional and personal conduct.
4   Applicants are required to pass a number of checks prior to their enrolment.
5   Failure to declare information that has a material influence on a student's fitness to practice may lead to termination of their medical course.

6 The practice of medicine requires the highest standards of professional competence.

7 The primary duty of care is to patients.

8 Applicants should demonstrate some understanding of what a career in medicine involves and their understanding of, and suitability for, a caring profession.

9 Medical Schools have agreed that the selection process for medical students must be transparent, involving procedures that respect obligations under relevant diversity and equality legislation.

i   *The Medical Schools Council, GUIDING PRINCIPLES FOR THE ADMISSION OF MEDICAL STUDENTS Revised March 2010*

ii   *Tomorrow's Doctors (2009). General Medical Council*

Make sure you visit:

www.gmc-uk.org General Medical Council – responsible for medical standards.
www.bma.org.uk British Medical Association – represents Doctors.
www.medschools.ac.uk – all UK medical schools.

Finally in this introduction we want to include these words from Anna Ehrlich, a student from JFS who didn't get in first time, but took a year out and got in second time around:

'I was very disappointed when I didn't get into medical school in year 13 despite 2 interviews. So I decided to persevere and apply again, and after working hard to get some A*s, I knew I had to get my interview technique up to scratch. First of all, I compiled a book with sections for the different types of questions that could be asked. I made extensive spider diagrams showing all the information regarding each medical school – not just why I loved their universities, but also about the course, local populations, endemic diseases, and the range of teaching hospitals (I was asked about all of these over the course of my 4 interviews this year). I made a section on ethics with notes on key or current ethical dilemmas, a section on the NHS, current news items, and the most common questions to remind myself of the key elements I wanted to get across in the interview. My final section involved analysing every sentence in my personal statement so that I was prepared to be asked on any of it. I found my book very helpful and I would recommend developing something similar. It helped me create a space for exploring my ideas, organised any facts I thought could be relevant, and was an aide-mémoire that I could visualise during interviews.

'Of course writing notes is only half of what is needed to prepare. Once you have read through your book, practising is key to reduce nerves for the real thing, structuring your answers and drawing on past experiences. Having a gap year allowed me to have time to experience a different country's health care system (I went to Ghana, but there are hospital volunteer projects worldwide), get hands on experience in an NHS hospital as a volunteer and obtain paid employment in childcare. Not only does this give you a topic of conversation in the interview, but you can also use what you have learned to back up answers to questions on other topics. For example, Barts & The London sent an article on Euthanasia pre-interview, and when discussing it on the day, I could speak about the suffering I had seen on the wards, including a patient who had considered suicide. This made me truly understand how desperate some patients feel and show the interviewers that I could see the patients and families perspectives, as well as the legal and ethical perspectives that I had researched. Drawing upon your experiences gives your answers depth, and shows the interviewers that you can reflect.

'Try to organise as many mock interviews as you can, and ask your interviewers to make it as realistic as possible (I had fifteen this year!). In the week leading up to your interview I would recommend: reading through the book you've made, discussing topics with family, talking through responses to common questions (while avoiding memorising word for word), and build up your enthusiasm for that medical school, even if it's your last choice. Being enthusiastic about medicine and the medical school is crucial – some medical schools even specify this on their website e.g. Newcastle. Although you will be nervous, you are well prepared, and you have got an interview which means you have a good chance of getting in – show them why they should want you in their medical school! Good luck!"

GWIST – A careers education framework for those applying to medicine:

Grades

Applicants need to know if the medicine degree that they are considering will really consider them with the grades that they have. The authors have concentrated on GCSEs, AS levels and A levels because this is what we know. We felt out of our comfort zone including detail on Scottish Highers, Welsh Bacc, International Baccalaureate and other possible entry qualifications. Hopefully there is enough detail in this chapter to still be helpful if you possess these qualifications or if you are a teacher, advisor or parent of someone who possesses these qualifications.

GCSEs

Medical schools seem to have three main approaches to GCSEs:

▸ There is an explicit stating that you must have a certain number of grades at A or A* (i.e. six As or five A*s) and if the applicant doesn't then they will not be considered further.

▸ They give an indication of what GCSE grades were average for applicants or successful applicants (i.e. seven A*s).

▸ The GCSE grades are expressed as a much lower minimum (i.e. six A–C) but it is soon made clear that, in the medical schools' holistic entry scoring process, if you possess (for medicine) weaker GCSE grades you will have to make up for it in other areas of entry criteria.

AS/A levels

While AAA for A level is the norm, we should note:

▸ The growth of the A*AA offer.

▸ A levels are more and more expected to be gained in the two years after GCSEs.

▸ The variation in what is expected from the 4th AS level – from nothing to an A.

▸ Varying policies on AS/A levels taken early.

Please browse the AS/A level requirements in the Rough Guide section to see all the differences.

The courses (that may involve a preliminary course) where you may be considered with less than AAA

Barts and London Queen Mary University of London (Newham residents only), Birmingham (local, contextual – A2B) – Bristol (contextual offer), Dundee (local, contextual), Keele (contextual – A2K), King's College London (A101 local, non-selective state school), Leeds (Access to Leeds-contextual, Bradford University Collaborative Programme), Liverpool and Lancaster (Access and Foundation routes – not usually for applicants with science A levels), Manchester (A104 contextual), Newcastle and Durham (Stage1 Biomolecular/Bioscience at Newcastle Transfer, Medicine Foundation-mature/health experience/contextual, A109 local/contextual), Norwich UEA (A104 contextual), Nottingham (A108 contextual), Sheffield (SOAMS contextual), Southampton (A102 contextual), St Andrews (Perth Pathway mature), St George's (contextual offer).

Criteria for these courses can vary tremendously so this is just a pointer.

Work Experience

Applicants should demonstrate some understanding of what a career in medicine involves and their understanding of, and suitability for, a caring profession. Applicants may draw on relevant work experience, either paid or voluntary in health or related areas, to demonstrate this understanding. Medical schools recognise that practical experience in hospices and residential homes, or domestic caring responsibilities, is equally appropriate as work in a conventional health care setting such as a hospital or GP surgery. More important than the experience itself, is the ability to demonstrate an understanding of the relevant skills and attributes the profession requires by reflecting upon and drawing on any experience they may have. Applicants should be advised that, in order to engage in health care related work experience, under vetting and barring legislation, they will be required to register with the appropriate body.

The Medical Schools Council, Guiding Principles for the Admission of Medical Students, Revised March 2010.

A common theme when looking at the published entry criteria, is that it is not essential to have hospital and GP experience as it is accepted that this is difficult to obtain. Reflection on what has been learned during the experience and relating this to personal qualities and qualities expected of doctors is extremely important. A browse through the different work experience criteria sections in the Rough Guide will soon make you aware of all the issues that need to be covered and this will help with personal statements, references and interviews.

It should be noted that medical schools are increasingly asking for verification of experiences mentioned in the personal statement. Applicants should keep a record of their experiences and ask if personnel at their experiences are happy with being put down as a referee. Verification could be in the form of referee confirmation in the UCAS reference or an applicant questionnaire, where the medical school may contact the work experiences directly. Try to think about the patients, cases or residents you may have met or observed. What do you now know that you didn't know before?

Interview

There now seem to be two main types of interview – panel interviews (sometimes called semi-structured interviews) and MMIs (multi-mini interviews). There are now some instances of group interviews being part of the process.

Some medical schools are looking for certain criteria to be met in interviews. This may give some clues for preparation. Look at the Rough Guide further on and then refer to current online information from the medical schools. Also read: *Medical School Interviews: A Practical Guide to Help You Get That Place at Medical School* by George Lee and Olivier Picard.

We visited two medical schools in London, one doing panel interviews and the other doing MMIs and noticed the following:

Panel Interview

▸ There was a three person panel – two health professionals (both GPs in this case) and a lay panel member (careers advisor).

▸ Interview lasted 15–20 minutes.

▸ Two panel members asked questions and one observed (this rotates after every interview).

▸ First panel member asks questions generally related to the personal statement; the second panel member asks supplementary questions including some based on BMAT part 3 essay.

▸ Questions will be different for every applicant.

▸ Applicant can ask questions at the end but it is not looked on unfavourably if they do not.

▸ Applicant is scored on a common scoring process – and the interview panel agree jointly to pass on their opinion to the admission team that the applicant should be rated as accepted, rejected or rated as borderline.

Multi-mini interviews (MMIs)

▸ MMIs are based on Objective Structured Clinical Examinations (OSCEs). OSCEs are designed to test performance and competence in skills such as clinical examination, communication and interpretation of results. They are commonly used in medical education. MMIs are usually OSCEs related to testing medical applicants against the core competences set out at the start of this chapter from the Medical Schools Council.

▸ There were seven assessors in each MMI session consisting of doctors, clinicians and at least one senior medical student assessing seven medical candidates. There was also an actor who is not involved in assessing the applicant.

▸ There were eight questions/tasks taking place in seven stations. The first station was a double session lasting ten minutes. The candidates then rotated around the stations clockwise, spending five minutes with each assessor answering only the question specific to each station.

▸ A recorded voice will say, 'You may now start the station'. Once they have done so the assessment will begin. It is signalled that candidates have thirty seconds remaining in each station.

▸ Assessors are not allowed to deviate from the questions or rephrase them. There is no small talk or comments.

▸ There is a common marking scheme and each assessor gives a global impression of excellent, acceptable and unacceptable.

▸ The atmosphere has the feeling of examination conditions.

Icebreaker question in all stations:

Why medicine?

Station 1
- Ethical dilemma

Station 2
- Work experience – what have you done and what are your reflections?

Station 3
- Medical research

Station 4
- Team working

Station 5
- Problem solving

Station 6
- Issues in health care

Station 7
- Scenario with actor

N.B. Some medical schools may ask you to sign a confidentiality clause!

Points of note:

Many questions you will face in interview will be some sort of version of:

▸ Why medicine?
▸ What have you learned from your work experience?
▸ What qualities do doctors need? And do you have them?
▸ What medical/health/policy related issues interest you and why?
▸ Ethical dilemma that you as an individual or the NHS as a whole may face?

Subject

Proving your interest in the subject through the personal statement

Medical schools may use the personal statement in a number of ways:

▸ It has to meet criteria set out in its admissions policy; if it does not, you will be rejected.
▸ It is marked against criteria and is then included in a holistic marking process.
▸ It is mainly used to prompt questions in the interview.
▸ It is not considered at all!

The applicant must take any criteria that are needed in terms of personal statements very seriously. The Rough Guide included here will be a useful starting point, followed by the medical schools' current online information.

Different medical schools may be looking for slightly different criteria in personal statements, so the applicant may have to write a personal statement that keeps all their medical schools happy.

Does your referee think you are suitable for the subject?

Sometimes there are guidelines for what is expected from the referee – see the Rough Guide further on. Sometimes the referee may not know that there are guidelines/criteria that need to be met so the applicant may need to point this out to them!

Some medical schools are asking for more than the 'school report' type of reference. They may also want the referee to verify work experience taken.

Understanding how the subject is studied – integrated, PBL (problem-based learning) or traditional?

N.B Sometimes it was not clear from the prospectus how the subject is taught and the authors have made a 'best guess' in the Rough Guide!

Traditional

Preclinical and clinical medicine are taught separately. All undergraduate preclinical students read for a life sciences degree on completing their first three years of study. The preclinical course will give you a very strong grounding in the medical sciences. You are essentially studying for a science degree at this stage.

Integrated

The majority of medical schools have adopted an integrated course. Courses are usually systems-based (e.g., cardiovascular, digestive) rather than discipline-based so you are learning material in a more holistic manner. The general trend is towards lectures and tutorials in the first couple of years, with formalised en masse teaching being replaced by ward-based teaching later in the course. There may also be some elements of problem-based learning included. Clinical exposure in the first years may just be visits to GPs and clinics and nothing more.

If early clinical exposure is important to you, do check out exactly what the course is offering and talk to current medical students. At one university open day I was told that early clinical exposure was a key feature, only to be told later by a medical student there that there was really very little of it!

Problem based learning (PBL)

According to the BMA 'in problem based learning (PBL) students use "triggers" from the problem case or scenario to define their own learning objectives. Subsequently they do independent, self-directed study before returning to the group to discuss and refine their acquired knowledge. Thus, PBL is not about problem solving per se, but rather it uses appropriate problems to increase knowledge and understanding. The process is clearly defined, and the several variations that exist all follow a similar series of steps.'

Students are split into groups and meet three/ four times a week to discuss one clinical scenario. The group, helped by a facilitator, will decide on learning objectives for that case (scientific knowledge, ethics, public health, statistics) and each student will do independent learning and then return to discuss what they have found. Students are not left to their own devices entirely as there are lectures (but significantly fewer than integrated courses) and clinical skills and communication sessions. As PBL courses rely on lots and lots of independent work, self-motivation and dedication to the course are extremely important. This approach is not for everybody.

Characteristics of PBL

▸ Student-centred PBL – It fosters active learning, improved understanding and retention and development of lifelong learning skills

▸ Generic competencies – PBL allows students to develop generic skills and attitudes desirable in their future practice

▸ Integration – PBL facilitates an integrated core curriculum

▸ Motivation – PBL is fun for students and tutors, and the process requires all students to be engaged in the learning process

▸ 'Deep' learning – PBL fosters deep learning (students interact with learning materials, relate concepts to everyday activities and improve their understanding)

▸ Constructivist approach – Students activate prior knowledge and build on existing conceptual knowledge frameworks and its disadvantages

▸ Tutors who can't 'teach' – Tutors enjoy passing on their own knowledge and understanding so may find PBL facilitation difficult and frustrating

▸ Human resources – More staff have to take part in the tutoring process

▸ Other resources – Large numbers of students need access to the same library and computer resources simultaneously

▸ Role models – Students may be deprived access to a particular inspirational teacher who in a traditional curriculum would deliver lectures to a large group

▸ Information overload – Students may be unsure how much self-directed study to do and what information is relevant and useful.

From the ABC of learning and teaching medicine: Problem based learning
www.bmj.com/cgi/reprint/326/7384/328.pdf.

Tests

The UKCAT and BMAT have now become extremely important in the process of applying to medicine. Failing to prepare for the tests is preparing to fail!

The authors are not looking to repeat information about the tests, which is easily available on the websites:

UKCAT: **www.ukcat.ac.uk**
BMAT: **www.admissionstestingservice.org/our-services/medicine-and-
         health care/bmat/about-bmat**

Bear in mind that:

▸   A few medical schools do not use a test.
▸   Some will have a cut-off score and if you fail to reach this then you will be rejected (some give a guide to their cut off score and some do not).
▸   Some medical schools only use the tests when applicants score equally on all other criteria.

In our experience we suggest a two-step process:

Step 1

In year 12, when the potential applicant has available time, go to the UKCAT website and do the two timed practice tests and go to the BMAT website and print off past papers and do them under timed conditions. With UKCAT keep doing them again and again, to help you get used to the timings. With BMAT you need to mark your papers yourself. You will have to make a judgement call on buying preparation books and preparation courses. Make this decision once you have taken some mock tests. Talk to advisors about this.

Step 2

You then need to look at the available information – see the Rough Guide and, more importantly, current online information. Are the scores that you are getting suitable for the courses that you are considering? Could you be applying for a course that you are highly likely to be rejected from because of your probable test result? Do not indulge in wishful thinking!

A rough guide to entry criteria for UK undergraduate medical degrees

The following information has been sourced from university prospectuses, medical school prospectuses, medical school admissions policies and other sundry documents available from online prospectuses such as FAQs.

We have ignored criteria such as CRB/DBS, health checks, etc.

*This information will become out of date very quickly (sourced January/February 2013). It is designed to make advisors, teachers, applicants and their parents aware of the complexities and idiosyncrasies of medical school entry criteria. It must never be used as a final reference source!

Aberdeen

Grades

GCSE

Grade C passes in English and Maths are required.

▸ Biology is recommended; Physics is recommended (or Dual Award Science).
▸ A combination of Grade A and B passes at GCSE is expected, especially in science subjects.

AS level

AS Level attainments currently do not form part of our academic requirements, as it is on A level achievement that any offer is made.

▸ AS module re-sits are permitted providing that the final three A levels are undertaken simultaneously over two years of study.

A levels

Achieve/Be predicted to achieve AAA in three A levels taken together at first sitting over a maximum of two years of study.

▸ Chemistry is required.
▸ One subject from Biology/Human Biology, Maths and Physics is required.
▸ One further A level in most other subjects. Check with the Medical Admissions Office if in doubt about the suitability of a subject.
▸ Combinations of Chemistry, Biology plus a Non-Science subject are as acceptable as all-science combinations.
▸ General Studies is not acceptable.

Work experience criteria

Relevant hospital or general practice experience is very useful, but there are often difficulties obtaining this. What we are looking for is an understanding of what a career in medicine entails, and that your perceptions aren't just based on *ER* or *Casualty*! In addition, you should list all your voluntary work activities and also paid employment, expanding on what you have learned from it in your personal statement.

*Do not use this information as a final reference source! Always check current online prospectuses as this information may not fully represent the holistic scoring process used, and could be out of date very quickly. This chapter is a one-stop shop, giving advisors and applicants a realistic idea of the range of criteria that needs to be met.

28

Check current online prospectus

Interview

The interview format at Aberdeen is to change from a two-person panel who question in three domains to a Multiple Mini Interview (MMI) format:

▸ Five candidates will be interviewed simultaneously.
▸ Each candidate will rotate around five separate questioning stations in turn.
▸ Each station will last seven minutes with one selector scoring performance against criteria.
▸ Individual stations will cover one domain or questioning area.
▸ Communication and interpersonal skills will also be scored at each station.

Subject – personal statement criteria

Assessed on:

Commitment to Medicine

The selectors want to satisfy themselves that applicants are highly committed, well informed and have adequately researched their future career (and medical school courses). This will include:

▸ Demonstration of attempts to experience the work of a doctor (the day-to-day involvement).
▸ Demonstration of attempts to research the training involved for a career in medicine (both at university and after qualifying).
▸ Demonstration of understanding of the level of commitment required (the 'highs' and 'lows' of being a doctor).

This can be achieved by:

▸ Job shadowing (observing GPs and/or hospital doctors at work).
▸ Talking with doctors (and medical students) about their lives, careers, future plans, etc.
▸ Attending open days and medical conferences/lectures.
▸ Consulting medical school websites/prospectuses.
▸ Reading literature regarding recent medical breakthroughs, newspaper headlines, etc.

Core Qualities of Doctors

Selectors want to see evidence of applicants' understanding of the core qualities of a doctor and thus their suitability for this career, e.g. demonstration of:

▸ Good communication skills.
▸ Evidence of concern for the welfare of others.
▸ Demonstration of being trustworthy and honest.

Applicants can strengthen an application by:

▸ Undertaking work of a caring nature.
▸ Undertaking work that benefits school colleagues.
▸ Personal experience of using 'people skills' in social/work situations.

Teamwork

Selectors need to know that applicants understand teamwork and strive to utilise their time in a constructive way, e.g. demonstrated by:

▸ activities at school
▸ activities out/with school
▸ attitude to colleagues
▸ ability to participate fully in school life and help others to do so
▸ school honours and prizes.

Subject – reference criteria

We do take note of what the teachers at school think of them, details of which may be mentioned in the reference. This could be whether students get on with their colleagues, complete work on time and are punctual and whether they contribute to school-based activities (e.g., choirs, orchestras, buddy system, charity fund-raising events, anti-bullying campaigns, etc).

Subject – how it is taught

Integrated

Test

UKCAT

The score allocated is based upon an applicant's overall performance in the UKCAT compared with the performance of all other applicants to Medicine at Aberdeen. Achievements are ranked in octiles and determine the appropriate score allocated.

Barts and the London Queen Mary University of London

Grades

GCSE

All eligible applicants must have the following subjects at GCSE level, at grades AAABBB or above (in any order) to include Biology (or Human Biology), Chemistry, English Language and Mathematics (or Additional Mathematics or Statistics). The Science double award may substitute all sciences at GCSE.

A levels/AS levels

AAAb from 3 A levels and 1 AS level

▸ Chemistry and Biology at AS level and at least one at A level. If both subjects not taken to A level, a second science A level is required. If you are planning to drop either Chemistry or Biology before A2, you must attain a B grade in that subject at AS level.
▸ If A level Maths and Further Maths are offered in the same sitting, Further Maths is acceptable at AS level only.
▸ General Studies and Critical Thinking are not accepted subjects at AS and A level.
▸ Our normal offer is for grades AAA in three A levels and B in the AS level.
▸ For candidates offering four A levels in two science and two non-science subjects, our normal offer is AAAC if no AS levels have been cashed in.

A levels achieved prior to Year 13 will be considered as part of the overall academic strength of an application but will not count towards an offer.

The medical school does not consider any applications from students who are re-sitting their AS or A level year thereby taking three years to achieve the required grades.

The School does accept AS re-sit modules taken within the two years of study.

Work experience criteria

We would expect that applicants will have undertaken some voluntary work experience in a caring/health environment and/or observation in a medical clinical setting. It is important for applicants to have a realistic appreciation of what a career as a health professional involves.

Interview

We always interview using a panel (that can contain tutors, admissions staff, doctors and current students) and are looking for the qualities that we consider would make you a good doctor. It would be useful to prepare yourself by looking at **admissionsforum.net** where you can find details of other students' experiences of interview.

Subject – personal statement criteria

No special mention is made on website

Subject – reference criteria

Reasons for rejection:

Your personal reference gave us doubts about your suitability for the course.

Subject – how it is taught

Problem-based learning

Test

How we use the UKCAT:
- For school-leavers/gap year students, you must achieve at least 2400 overall in the UKCAT.
- We are not able to give you advice on the minimum score we require, since it varies from year to year, however, it is unlikely that you would be offered an interview if you obtained a TOTAL UKCAT score below 2400. There is no guarantee you will be offered an interview if you score above this.

Birmingham

Grades

GCSEs

Normally, applicants must offer A* grades in each of English (either English Language or English Literature), Mathematics and all science subjects. Integrated Science (double certificate) is acceptable as an alternative to single sciences.

Overall GCSE performance will be considered.

AS/A Level

A*AA; Predicted results: Normally AAA.

All A2 modules of three subjects must be undertaken in Year 13.

Chemistry and Biology (or Human Biology) required.

Check current online prospectus

If third subject is Psychology, Sociology, Physical Education, Theatre Studies, Dance, Art or Music, a fourth academic subject at AS is required.

Certificated as well as non-certificated results must be provided (the latter could be included in the reference).

Preference will be given to those applicants who offer AAAA, achieved by the end of the first year of A level study. Mathematics and Further Mathematics will not be considered as separate subjects.

Work experience criteria

In deciding who to invite for interview, academic excellence is not the only criterion. It is equally important to be able to demonstrate that you are well-motivated towards a career in medicine especially through volunteering and/or work experience. You should also use your time on work experience effectively by gaining insight into the demands placed on staff, the problems they encounter and the strategies that they employ to handle difficult situations as well as the benefits they obtain from caring for people and working in teams. Again, opportunities to engage in discussion of these issues must be taken.

Interview

Interviews are organised in a multiple mini-interview format. You will participate in four separate, short interviews, lasting six minutes each. This will allow you to start afresh at each mini-interview. A range of your personal attributes relevant to studying medicine will be assessed by means of different tasks. Interview stations are designed to assess aspects such as: motivation for medicine, communication, self-insight, ethical reasoning, scientific understanding and interpretation.

Interactive Task: In a role play scenario, the interview candidate will be expected to negotiate with a fourth year medicine student. Both the candidate and the student are playing themselves in the role play. An interviewer will observe the interaction.

Motivation and Insight: The candidate will be asked about work experience but in a very focused way.

Data Interpretation: This station will consider a published study. A graph and or a table from the study is provided and the candidate is asked to interpret these data and also to perform straightforward arithmetic calculations.

Dealing with Difficulty and Doing the Right Thing: The candidate is asked about events from their life and is also presented with a hypothetical ethical dilemma relating to studying medicine.

Subject – personal statement criteria

In addition, we want to ensure that you possess other qualities required of a potential doctor. Therefore, extracurricular involvement is important in addition to the work experience. Evidence of on-going activities involving significant interactions with a broad range of people in a responsible capacity is a relevant aspect. Activities that take place outside of school are especially appreciated.

Subject – how it is taught

Integrated

Test

No test

Check current online prospectus

Brighton and Sussex Medical School

Grades

GCSE

When we look at GCSEs, we are primarily interested in the A and A* grades and so the more of these you have the better. However, strong AS grades (where appropriate) will compensate for a weaker GCSE profile. Please note that, for all applicants, we expect grades B in GCSE Maths & English (or their equivalent).

AS/A Level

Most standard offers for entry to BSMS are conditional on gaining three A grades at A level, following the study of at least four subjects to AS level. Both Biology and Chemistry must have been studied to A level and passed with a minimum A grade. We do not specify the nature of the third A level subject but it should be noted that neither General Studies nor Critical Thinking are acceptable at any level.

BSMS will consider re-sit applicants. However, due the large number of applications that we receive, we will ordinarily only consider applications from individuals who have slipped a grade in one subject and obtained a B (plus two A grades). You will be required to be predicted, and subsequently to attain, an A in the subject that you are re-taking to be eligible for consideration. Anyone who has missed our offer level by more than this, or who is not predicted an A at retake, is strongly advised to consider the route of taking a BSc degree and then, with a high 2.1 Honours or better, applying as a graduate, either to a five year course or to a four year graduate entry programme.

Work experience criteria

In assessing your application BSMS admissions tutors will be seeking evidence of:
▸   a realistic attitude to medical training and clinical practice
▸   a commitment to caring for others
▸   the ability to communicate and work effectively within a team
▸   the ability to appreciate other people's point of view
▸   a willingness to accept responsibility.

Please note that BSMS may verify references and records of work experience and you will be asked, if called for interview, to bring with you documentary evidence of any work experiences undertaken.

Interview
▸   A formal 20 minute semi-structured interview

Subject – personal statement criteria

In assessing your application BSMS admissions tutors will be seeking evidence of:
▸   academic achievement and potential
▸   a realistic attitude to medical training and clinical practice
▸   a commitment to caring for others
▸   the ability to communicate and work effectively within a team
▸   the ability to appreciate other people's point of view
▸   a willingness to accept responsibility.

Subject – how it is taught

Integrated – also read about Mobile Medical Education Initiative

Test

All applicants to BSMS are required to take the UKCAT the summer prior to applying to us. However, there is currently no threshold. We only use the UKCAT once you have been interviewed, either if you are on borderline with other candidates to being offered a place here, or if you are already on our waiting list and a space has become available. A low UKCAT score does not mean that your application will automatically be made unsuccessful if you meet our other entry requirements.

Bristol

Grades

GCSE

We look for good grades in a wide spread of subjects. Non-graduate students (sixth form applicants) must achieve at least five subjects at grade A to include Mathematics, English Language and the sciences. Graduates must achieve grade B in Mathematics, English Language and two sciences (or double award science). Credit is given to grades at A/A* up to a maximum of eight subjects.

AS/A level

You will need to achieve AAA at A2 level including an A in chemistry and one other laboratory-based science subject (general studies and critical thinking are not approved subjects and are not included in offers). They should be certificated at the same sitting, at the first attempt and completed in two years. You should be aware that if you are offering three A2 levels, the choice of subjects should avoid undue overlap of content. The combinations Biology and Physical Education or Biology and Sports Science are not accepted. Currently, we do not have minimum requirements for AS level and accept re-sit modules, but not A2 level re-sits. We require a minimum of grade C to be achieved in the 4th AS level subject, but we do not otherwise look at the AS results. We require the A level grades to be achieved in one sitting and within two years. We accept module re-sits within the two years but not outside of the two years.

Work experience criteria

You should try to gain as wide voluntary experience as possible in a caring or health environment. This does not have to be in a hospital (that can be difficult to obtain; a nursing home, local hospice, shelter for the homeless, working with people with disabilities or special needs, or working with a youth group would all be useful experience.

Interview

The interviews last for 15 to 20 minutes and are conducted by two interviewers. You will be asked questions such as why you want to study medicine, what you know about the course and career and what recent developments in medicine you have read about.

Check current online prospectus

Criteria for assessing the candidate's performance at interview:
a)   why they wish to study medicine and attributes
b)   ability to communicate
c)   self-confidence and enthusiasm
d)   evidence of extramural activities
e)   awareness of current developments
f)   ability to develop coherent stance on a topical subject
g)   informed about University and course
h)   informed about career
i)   overall impression created by candidate.

Subject – personal statement criteria

Has the candidate:
1   a realistic interest in Medicine?
2   informed him/herself about a career in Medicine?
3   demonstrated a commitment to helping others?
4   demonstrated a wide range of interests?
5   contributed to school/college/community activities?
6   a range of personal achievements (excluding exams)?

Each of these is scored on a four-point scale.

For detailed information on what each criterion includes and how it can be evidenced in your personal statement, see the Entry Profile on the UCAS website, **www.ucas.com** (via course search).

Subject – reference criteria

References are read in conjunction with the personal statement and used as supporting information. Candidates with an adverse comment from their referee are unlikely to be successful.

Subject – how it is taught

The course is traditional with the first teaching in years one and two being a series of lectures, tutorials and practicals.

Test

Bristol does not currently require any of these tests. We select applicants on the basis of the UCAS form and then interview approximately the top 20% of applicants.

Cambridge

Grades

GCSE

Students wishing to study Medicine must obtain grade C or above in GCSE (or equivalent) Double Award Science and Mathematics. Two single awards in GCSE Biology and Physics may be substituted for Double Award Science.

Do not use this information as a final reference source! Always check current online prospectuses as this information may not fully represent the holistic scoring process used, and could be out of date very quickly. This chapter is a one-stop shop, giving advisors and applicants a realistic idea of the range of criteria that needs to be met.

35

Check current online prospectus

AS/A levels

A*AA

Applicants must have AS or A level passes in Chemistry and two of Biology/Human Biology, Physics and Mathematics.

At least one pass must be at A level, although most applicants for Medicine at Cambridge have at least three science/mathematics A levels and some Colleges require this or ask for particular A level subject(s). See individual College websites for details.

Although many Colleges consider applicants offering only two science/mathematics subjects at A level, please note that the success rate of such applicants is much lower. In the past three admissions rounds, 97% of applicants for Medicine (A100) offered three or more science/mathematics A levels and, of these, 21% were successful in obtaining a place. Of the 3% of applicants who offered only two science/mathematics A levels, just 3% were successful in gaining a place.

Please note that in the following 'science/mathematics subjects' refers to Biology/Human Biology, Chemistry, Physics and Mathematics. It does not include Psychology.

On the supplementary application questionnaire it states – For each unit you have taken, please provide details of the unit code, unit title, date taken, UMS (Uniform Mark Score) score achieved, maximum UMS score possible and indicate whether you plan to retake it. Please note that UMS scores should be listed for each sitting of the unit and regardless of whether or not you have certificated or retaken the unit. Please note that you may be asked to bring evidence of the UMS scores you have achieved with you if you are invited to attend an interview.

Work experience criteria

Students are referred to – *The Medical Schools Council, GUIDING PRINCIPLES FOR THE ADMISSION OF MEDICAL STUDENTS, Revised March 2010* – point eight.

Interview

You will have one, two or three interviews (most commonly two), each lasting from twenty to forty-five minutes. How many interviews you will have depends on the College to which you applied or were allocated. However, you'll be told what to expect in advance.

Interviews are predominantly academic and subject-related. One or two will be with specialists in the subject you've applied for, one of whom is usually the Director of Studies (who oversees your academic studies at Cambridge). There may be another more general interview with someone not directly related to your subject, probably a college admissions tutor – the person in charge of admissions for that College.

Subject – personal statement criteria

None specifically mentioned

Subject – how it is taught

Traditional with supervisions

Test

BMAT – applicants who score in the bottom half of the BMAT spectrum may not be called for interview, especially if their AS Level performance is marginal.

Cardiff

Grades

GCSE

Mathematics B, English Language B and Sciences AAB or AA (Double Award)

▸ As a guide we advise applicants that you will need to achieve four to five A*s in 9 GCSEs for your application to meet the minimum threshold, which is set each year once all applications are received. Please remember that we have to include your Maths, English Language and Sciences grades in those 9, even if you have higher grades in other subjects. Once we have looked at our required subjects, we will then look at your top grades from your remaining GCSEs.

When your application comes in, the first thing we do is score the top 9 GCSEs achieved.

▸ These 9 GCSEs must include English Language, the Sciences and Maths.
▸ You will get 3 points for an A*, 2 points for an A and 1 point for a B.
▸ You can score a maximum of 27 points.
▸ We do not count short courses as part of this assessment.

After this you are allocated an academic score. When all of the applications for the cycle are scored, a cut-off score is decided and only applicants who meet this threshold will go on to the non-academic stage of the process. Last year we were looking for a minimum of 25 academic points, which works out at about 7 A*s on average. We do not know in advance what the cut off score will be; it is dependent on the number of applicants that there were in that cycle and the scores that they have achieved.

AS/A level

AAA in at least two sciences out of Biology, Chemistry, Maths and Statistics (one of which must be Biology or Chemistry) and a minimum of a grade C in a fourth AS Level (Grade A if Biology or Chemistry)

▸ For applicants offering two or more Mathematics and/or Statistics subjects at AS and/or A2 level, only one will count towards meeting the conditions of an offer. Further Maths is not accepted at AS or A2 level.
▸ General Studies is not accepted and Critical Thinking is only accepted at AS level.
▸ We welcome students with a broad range of studies and therefore your third A level subject does not have to be science related.

Work experience criteria

You will be scored on an insight into a career in medicine

Interview

Panel interview (two or three people)

Subject – personal statement and reference criteria

Applicants who meet the minimum academic requirements and are sufficiently highly ranked academically are assessed on non-academic criteria according to the information contained in their personal statement and the Referee's Report given on the UCAS application form.

Applications are reviewed by trained selectors and the following are assessed and scored:

▸ insight into a career in Medicine

▸ evidence of experience and reflection in a caring environment

▸ evidence and reflection of personal responsibility

▸ evidence of a balanced approach to life

▸ evidence of self-directed learning.

Subject – how it is taught

Integrated

Test

Yes, all applicants must sit the UKCAT test. There is no minimum score or threshold required for Cardiff in the UKCAT so no matter what you apply with, we will still consider your application. We only use the results of an applicant's UKCAT test if we are at the end of the process with two applicants in a 'tiebreak' situation, at which point we may refer to the test results to make a decision.

Dundee

Grades

GCSE

Achievement at GCSE and AS level will be taken into account.

Biology is required, at least to GCSE level.

AS/A Level

AAA grades at A level (A2), to include Chemistry and another Science. The third subject can be your own choice; we have no preference.

These results should be obtained at one sitting and at the first attempt at A level examinations, two years after GCSE.

Work experience criteria

Work experience allows applicants to gain some experience of a career in health care. This may include working with people who may be ill, disabled or elderly as well as by shadowing a doctor. The selectors recognise that not all applicants will have the same opportunities to gain such experience, but expect everyone to be informed about their career choice. In general terms they look for work experience lasting two weeks (or equivalent) and do not encourage more than this.

Interview

The University of Dundee divides its medical school interview process into a series of 10 seven-minute 'mini interviews'. The usual topics are covered but within bite-size sections rather than a single discussion that offers you a number of separate opportunities to sell yourself. You can expect to be asked about your understanding of: a medical career, the curriculum here in Dundee, aspects of your UCAS statement as well as current medical issues in the press, including ethical topics. In addition we will be looking to assess your communication skills and approach towards teamwork through a series of interactive stations where you have a task to complete or actor to talk to.

Do not use this information as a final reference source! Always check current online prospectuses as this information may not fully represent the holistic scoring process used, and could be out of date very quickly. This chapter is a one-stop shop, giving advisors and applicants a realistic idea of the range of criteria that needs to be met.

Check current online prospectus

Subject – personal statement criteria

Must also complete an online survey!

From 2013 cycle information on non-academic achievements and references will not be considered until interview. Thereafter, we aim to rate applications as fairly as possible based upon the various forms of other evidence that is presented on the UCAS form. There is no ideal formula and we would not wish to promote particular activities. Hence we consider these under separate headings, which receive equal weight. Some examples are given below but this list is not exclusive or exhaustive. The selectors will consider achievement in all areas and prefer evidence in more than one area. Non-academic achievements will be discussed at interview and we may seek confirmation of these at our discretion:

▸ Competitive achievement – e.g. chess or sport at national level or above

▸ talents – music, drama, public speaking, leadership qualities

▸ social responsibility – voluntary work, teamwork, youth organisations

▸ employment – entrepreneurial, sustained engagement, achievement.

Subject – how it is taught

Integrated

Test

Your UKCAT score will be factored into the pre-interview rank. There is no specific cut off applied but obviously a high score is advantageous. Our analysis of the 2010 applicants revealed that we interviewed few applicants with a UKCAT score below 2300 and the average for those gaining offers was more than 2600.

Edinburgh

Grades

GCSE

The average A level applicant is offering 6A*s at GCSE and the top one third (around 350) between 8 and 11 A*. GCSEs: Grade B in Biology, Chemistry, English, Mathematics. Double Award Combined Sciences or equivalent at Grade BB may replace GCSE grades in sciences. Additional Applied Sciences or Applied Science will not be accepted.

AS/A level

AAA in Upper Sixth including Chemistry plus Grade B at AS level in a fourth subject. A levels must include Chemistry and one of Biology, Mathematics or Physics. Biology at AS Level required as minimum. For both AS and A level, only one of Mathematics or Further Mathematics will be considered. Human Biology may replace Biology but General Studies will not be considered. Those applying with re-sit qualifications (other than GCE AS levels) will not be entered into the selection system unless under very exceptional circumstances (for which verified evidence has been provided prior to UCAS application).

Do not use this information as a final reference source! Always check current online prospectuses as this information may not fully represent the holistic scoring process used, and could be out of date very quickly. This chapter is a one-stop shop, giving advisors and applicants a realistic idea of the range of criteria that needs to be met.

39

Work experience criteria

We do not specify a length of time and we do not assess this on your application. We need you to gain experience of the diseased, disadvantaged and disabled. This can have been through one or many experiences. We also look at what you have obtained from your experience. It is important you are as sure as you can be that medicine is the right choice for you. You don't want to find out once you start the course that you faint at the sight of blood! Demonstration of a clear understanding of the nature of a career of medicine will be expected. This can be achieved by appropriate work experience or work shadowing, as evidence of an informed decision to apply for a medical programme, such as talking with medical doctors and medical students, attending a university open day and medical conferences/lectures, reading medical literature.

The Admissions Committee recognises that not all applicants have equal opportunities to gain such experience. If it is not possible to get any work experience in a hospital then other alternatives include working in a nursing home, riding for the disabled or volunteer work.

Interview

School leavers are not usually interviewed

Subject – personal statement and reference criteria

The non-academic criteria score will take the following into account:

▶ Personal qualities and skills, empathy, interpersonal relationships and ability to communicate.

▶ Evidence of career exploration prior to application, understanding of medicine, work experience and shadowing (diseased, disadvantaged and disabled).

▶ Breadth and level of non-academic achievements and interests: social involvement, school responsibilities, leadership, organisational abilities, cultural, sporting, vocational and voluntary achievements, interests and hobbies.

Subject – how it is taught

Problem-based learning

Test

We do not have a cut-off score for UKCAT. We will accept any score you achieve.

The Selection Committee uses your UKCAT score to make a more informed decision about your application. Once all the scores are received we rank them into four quartiles, using the total UKCAT score rather than the average. Those applicants whose UKCAT scores come in the top quartile are allocated three points, second quartile are allocated two points, third quartile are allocated one point and the fourth quartile are not allocated any points. The points are then added to your total score to contribute towards your final ranking. Test results are worth 8% of the overall score of an application. The score an applicant actually achieved may be taken into consideration when final decisions are being made and there are a number of applicants with the same ranked score and limited places left to offer.

Exeter (new for 2013)

Grades

GCSE/AS/A levels

AAA–AAA*

GCE AL Chemistry and either Biology or Physics. Biology must be achieved at a minimum of Grade C at AS level if not studied at AL. Four subjects must be studied at AS level. General Studies is not included in any offer.

Work experience criteria

None mentioned

Subject – personal statement criteria

None mentioned

Subject – how it is taught

PBL/Integrated

Test

UKCAT

Glasgow

Grades

GCSE/AS/A level

AAA in three A2 examinations at one sitting to include Chemistry and one from Biology, Maths or Physics. General studies is *not* acceptable as a third subject at A2. A GCSE pass in English at a minimum of Grade B is also required. If Biology is not studied at A2 level, it should be taken at AS level. Grade A is required.

Work experience criteria

Although specific work experience in a hospital or general practice is not essential, it is important for all applicants to find out about the realities of a career in medicine. Work experience in a medical setting is not necessary to study medicine but it is expected that candidates will have at least spoken to a doctor such as their own GP about a career in medicine or have found out about a medical career through reading careers books or newspapers. An awareness of current issues facing the medical profession is also expected, which can be obtained from newspapers, journals and the Internet. An interest in caring for others is also expected, which can be demonstrated through voluntary/paid work in a community setting.

Interview

You may be invited to attend an interview

Check current online prospectus

Subject – personal statement criteria

See notes on work experience

Subject – how it is taught

Integrated

Test

Depending on the number of applications the Medical School receives by 15 October and the range of UKCAT scores received in November, the Medical School may not be in a position to consider further all applicants who meet/are predicted to achieve minimum academic entry requirements and who also possess the UKCAT national average total score.

Interviewees who meet/are predicted to achieve the minimum academic entry requirements will be ranked by UKCAT total score. Allocations for interviews will then be processed from the top UKCAT total score.

Hull York

Grades

GCSE

GCSE English Language at grade A.

We will accept grade B only if:

you have GCSE English Literature at grade A, or you are a school-leaver and you have AS level or A level English Literature or English Language at grade B. We will not accept any other subject as evidence of your English language ability.

GCSE Maths at grade A.

We will accept grade B only if:

you are a school-leaver and you have AS level or A level Maths at grade B.

We will not accept any other subject as evidence of your maths ability.

Six other GCSEs at grades A–C.

AS/A level

Our typical offer is AAA at A2, achieved in a single sitting, including Biology and Chemistry. If you apply to HYMS in your A2 year, you must be predicted at least AAB for us to consider your application. For the third A2 subject, we consider all subjects of equal merit except General Studies, Applied Science or Critical Thinking.

You will also need a fourth subject at AS level grade B (not General Studies, Citizenship or Critical Thinking).

Taking an A level early – we won't accept an A level taken in Year 11 or earlier. However, if you have achieved grade A in an A level in Year 12, we will accept this as one of the three grade As we require at A2 (that must include Biology and Chemistry). This will replace the requirement for you to have a fourth subject at AS level grade B.

If you do this, you must still be taking three A levels to A2 in Year 13, and any offer made to you will be conditional on achieving AAB in those subjects in Year 13. Also, each A level you offer must have taken no more than two years to complete.

Other A level elements

Undertaking the Extended Project (EP) won't be a condition of our offer, but we recognise that it will provide you with the opportunity to develop research and academic skills that are relevant for our course.

You can also offer a single vocational A level in Health and Social Care or IT, or a distinction in a single level 3 BTEC award or certificate, in combination with Biology and Chemistry A levels.

We don't normally accept results from re-sits taken in a third year of post-sixteen education.

Work experience criteria

There is no prescribed pre-application experience for applicants to HYMS, but you should try to obtain a realistic understanding of the demands of medical training and practice. You will find it useful to get some experience in a range of caring situations, observing or working alongside health care staff, in either a voluntary or paid capacity.

We also advise that you explore both the positive and negative aspects of a medical career through talking to doctors and other health care professionals. We will expect you to demonstrate that you understand, and are committed to, teamwork and the social context of health care.

Interview

You will normally be interviewed by two people, typically one female and one male, one of whom is typically an experienced clinician and one of whom may be a current HYMS medical student. Your interviewers will not have seen your UCAS form, because the interview explores different attributes that are not well assessed from a written application.

Your interview will last about twenty minutes. It will be formally structured, with a fixed number of questions. One question will be based on an article that you will be given to read immediately beforehand. The article will be short and non-technical, of the type you might find in a broadsheet newspaper.

The other questions will explore the following attributes:
▸ knowledge and understanding of problem-based learning
▸ motivation for medicine
▸ depth and breadth of interests, knowledge and reflection about medicine and the wider world
▸ teamwork and work experience
▸ personal insight – knowledge of own strengths and weaknesses
▸ understanding of the role of medicine in society
▸ tolerance of uncertainty and ambiguity.

Subject – personal statement and reference criteria

Using a standard assessment sheet, we score your UCAS form out of a maximum of twenty-five points. We assess the level of evidence you provide for each of the following personal attributes:
▸ motivation for medicine
▸ a realistic understanding of medicine, including hands-on experience of caring and observing health care in hospital and community settings

Do not use this information as a final reference source! Always check current online prospectuses as this information may not fully represent the holistic scoring process used, and could be out of date very quickly. This chapter is a one-stop shop, giving advisors and applicants a realistic idea of the range of criteria that needs to be met.

- self-motivation and responsibility
- communication skills
- ability to work with others
- other unusual qualities or life-experience.

When writing about your work experience, we look not only for a list of what you've done but also for your reflections on what you learned about yourself, or the medical profession, from that experience.

Our selection procedure ensures that any declared disability or criminal conviction is not allowed to influence the UCAS form assessment.

If we find out that any of the information on your UCAS form is untrue or misleading, you may forfeit your offer or place at HYMS.

All UCAS forms that meet our minimum academic criteria are read and scored by a trained HYMS assessor.

We consider your personal statement and your reference together as one document. We don't consider unsolicited references or any additional information, except for evidence of mitigating circumstances.

Subject – how it is taught

Problem-based learning

Test

All our applicants must take the UKCAT in the year they apply. We award you a number of points depending on your UKCAT score, and add this to the points from your UCAS form to give the total score, which we use to rank you against other applicants.

If you have a total UKCAT score of less than 2200 or a score of less than 450 in any of the four cognitive subtests, your application won't normally be considered. If you meet these minimum requirements, we will award you up to 25 points based on your UKCAT score, as follows:

UKCAT score	Points awarded
2200–2399	5
2400–2599	10
2600–2799	15
2800–2999	20
3000+	25

Imperial College

Grades

GCSE

All applicants must have the following subjects at GCSE level, at grades AAABB or above (in any order): Biology (or Human Biology), Chemistry, English Language, Mathematics (or Additional Mathematics or Statistics), Physics. The Science double award may substitute all sciences at GCSE.

AS/A level

Minimum entry requirements for this course are three A levels, including Chemistry and/or Biology and one science or mathematics subject, and one additional subject at AS level. If either Chemistry or Biology is offered alone at A level, then the other is required at AS level with at least a grade B.

Our normal offer is for grades AAA in three A levels and B in the AS level. The three A levels must be undertaken in the same academic year. For candidates offering four A levels our normal offer is AAAC. Vocational A and AS levels are not acceptable and general studies will not be accepted at any level.

Work experience criteria

Work experience for potential medical students should give them a realistic understanding of what is involved in a career in medicine and thus be a sound basis upon which to decide whether such a career would suit them. Imperial is unlikely to offer places to candidates who have not gained such an understanding. Candidates may also be asked to provide written documentation by way of evidence in support of their most recent and/or substantial work experience.

However, we appreciate that it can be difficult to obtain work experience in hospitals and GP surgeries, particularly without the help of your school or a medically qualified friend or relative. If this is your situation, we recommend you look for experience as a care assistant or volunteer in a nursing or residential home, or as a volunteer in a hospital or other community establishment. Similarly, although we would like to see a sustained commitment, we understand that this is not always possible. You should expect the interview panel to explore what you have gained from your work experience.

Interview

If selected, you will be required to attend a fifteen-minute interview. Normally interview panels consist of a chairperson, two other members of the selection panel, a senior medical student and frequently a lay observer. The interview is not intended to be an intimidating experience and staff will try to put candidates at ease while evaluating the following:

▸ Motivation and realistic approach to medicine as a career
▸ Capacity to deal with stressful situations
▸ Evidence of working as both a leader and a team member
▸ Ability to multitask
▸ Likely contribution to university life
▸ Communication skills and maturity of character.

Subject – personal statement criteria

If a candidate fulfils the minimum entry requirements and has scores in the top rankings for all three sections of BMAT, his or her application form will be passed to an experienced member of the selection panel. The selection panel comprises teachers in undergraduate education with experience in the admissions process, who will decide whether to offer the candidate an interview. These decisions are ratified by one of the admissions tutors. The panel members look at the following criteria when assessing applications:

GCSE results, A/AS level or equivalent predicted (or achieved) grades, BMAT scores, Motivation and understanding of medicine as a career, Community activities, Leadership and teamwork, General interests, Referee's report.

Subject – how it is taught

Integrated

Test

Invitations to an interview will be based on the content of your UCAS application and your performance in all three sections of BMAT. BMAT cut-off scores are calculated each year, as a result of ranked candidate BMAT scores versus number of expected interview sessions. As a result, the absolute BMAT cut-off changes each year. However, the BMAT cut-off scores from previous admissions cycles may be used as a guide. For 2012 entry, a score of 4.9 in each of sections 1 and 2, coupled with a score of 2.5 and grade C in section 3, were the minimum scores required.

Keele

Grades

GCSE

We require a minimum of four GCSE subjects at grade A, not including short-course GCSEs. Mathematics, English Language, Biology, Chemistry and Physics must be passed at a minimum of grade B. GCSE Science/Core Science (including AQA Science A or Science B) plus Additional Science is acceptable as an alternative to Biology, Chemistry and Physics; Applied Science is not an acceptable GCSE. IGCSE double-award Science is also acceptable.

AS/A Level

The standard offer for school-leavers will be 3 A levels at grades AAA or A*AB (with no grade below B), plus a minimum of grade B in the fourth AS.

AS level grades should be declared in the application.

Biology or Chemistry plus another designated science subject (Biology, Chemistry, Physics or Maths/Further Maths) and a third rigorous academic subject. There is no requirement for an A* or A grade to be achieved in a specific subject. Only one subject from a combination of Maths with Further Maths or Biology/Human Biology with Physical Education will be considered within the three A Levels, although the other subject may be offered as a fourth AS level. If only two sciences are offered, the science subjects not offered at AS/A level are required at GCSE grade B or above.

We require a minimum of three A levels plus a fourth AS to be completed within two years.

From 2012, achieved AS grades will be taken into account when assessing applicants' academic performance. In addition, chemistry AS level must be passed at a minimum of grade B if not taken at A2. If three A levels have been achieved, a fourth AS is required at a minimum of grade B. If four A levels have been achieved at the required grades, no further AS requirements will apply. An Extended Project Qualification (EPQ) will be considered in place of the fourth AS.

Applicants are reminded that all qualifications that have been completed must be declared in the UCAS application. If we find that an applicant has deliberately withheld AS grades, her/his application will be cancelled and she/he will be reported to UCAS.

All applications are first read by our Admissions Team to ensure that you meet the minimum academic requirements. If you do not meet these your application will be rejected at this initial stage.

Work experience and subject – personal statement/reference criteria

If academic requirements are met, applications will be given an academic score and passed to our Admissions Tutors.

Admissions Tutors assess your UCAS application for information on the following areas:

▸ understanding of the role of a doctor
▸ examples of regular hands-on caring work experience
▸ depth of experience in a role involving personal interaction
▸ reflection on what was learned from these experiences
▸ initiative/enterprise
▸ work/life balance
▸ working in teams
▸ communication (particularly outside your peer group)
▸ quality of written application.

They will pay particular attention to your personal statement and to the reference from your school/college.

You should ensure that this information is given to the person who will complete your reference. Both you and your referee should address each aspect outlined above. Referees should be aware that we expect to see more than a record of academic achievement. References indicating your strengths in the areas listed above are much more valuable than simple 'school report' – style references.

Interview

Each (chosen) candidate will have a similar structured multiple mini-interview.

Subject – how it is taught

Problem-based learning

Test

Keele uses UKCAT results only in borderline cases. Those applicants who narrowly miss achieving the required score for their UCAS application will receive further consideration (usually in the form of second-marking) if they have a total UKCAT score in the top 50% nationally. Applicants holding offers who narrowly miss achieving the required grades in their A levels (or equivalent level-3 qualification) may receive further consideration if there are places available. In these circumstances, the factors taken into consideration in allocating remaining places will include interview score and UKCAT score.

Applicants receiving offers for 2012 entry had UKCAT total scores ranging from 2020 to 3070.

King's College London

Grades

GCSE

At least grade B at English Language and Maths, if not offered at A/AS level.

AS/A level

3 A levels and one AS level
AAA at A level plus B at AS level
2 A levels and three AS level
AA at A level plus AAB at AS level

Compulsory subjects:

Chemistry and Biology, at least one at A level, the other must be at AS level.

Work experience and subject – personal statement/reference criteria

▸ Scholastic activities (Very Desirable).
▸ Any scholastic activity would be considered, eg general reading, debating, theological interests, etc.
▸ Community activities (Very Desirable).
▸ We look for applicants who have participated as fully as possible in school, college or community life, making the most of the opportunities available to them and also demonstrated some experience of society beyond their immediate environment. Your interests, achievements and contribution to your community are taken into account, e.g., clubs, theatrical, religious, etc.
▸ General activities/interests (Very Desirable).
▸ We look for applicants who not only have interests but may have also achieved in these areas e.g., music, sport, first aid, etc.
▸ Work shadowing/observation (Very Desirable).
▸ We would normally expect that applicants will have undertaken some voluntary work experience in a caring/health environment and/or observation in a medical clinical setting. It is important for applicants to have a realistic appreciation of what a career as a health professional involves.
▸ Paid or voluntary work (Very Desirable).
▸ Any voluntary contribution to your community is taken into account, eg volunteer in a care home. We look for evidence that you have worked in a setting where you can interact with the general public e.g., in a pharmacy, check-out or restaurant.
▸ We would expect your referee to be able to confirm your academic achievements and potential, and your character and suitability for medicine.

Interview

Normally, a semi-structured interview, usually fifteen to twenty minutes, with at least two interviewers. Interviewees complete a short questionnaire.

Subject – how it is taught

Integrated

Test

UKCAT

Lancaster

Grades

GCSE

Students need GCSEs in 9 subjects with a score of at least fifteen points from these nine subjects (where A*/A = 2 points, B = 1 point). Students must have at least a B in Maths, English Language and Science (either Core and Additional Science or Physics, Chemistry and Biology).

AS/A Level

Minimum of AAA(b).

Chemistry and Biology are subject requirements at A2 level. General studies and critical thinking only considered as the fourth subject. Only one of Maths or Further Maths will be considered. The extended project qualification may be acceptable at grade B in place of the AS level qualification in some instances.

Work experience criteria

Candidates must demonstrate suitable evidence of:
▸ health care career awareness/insight
▸ a caring contribution to the local community
▸ a critical, coherent and informative approach to written communication.

Interview

The interview process for entry to study medicine at Lancaster has consisted of a Multiple Mini Interview (MMI). The MMI consists of twelve different 'stations', most of which will be five minutes long. Some of the stations will consist of a short interview, where you will be asked questions related to your career choice. At others, you may be asked to read a short paragraph or watch a short video clip, take notes and then discuss at a subsequent station. One station will involve group work and will assess your suitability for our problem-based learning curriculum. Applicants who are selected for interview will be sent more detailed information nearer the time.

Subject – personal statement criteria

LMS staff assess your personal statement and those applicants who have most ably demonstrated that they possess the appropriate experience, aptitudes and communication skills will be invited to attend for interview.

Subject – how it is taught

Problem-based learning

Test

No, UKCAT is not part of our entry requirements.

N.B.: (as at early 2013)

Lancaster Medical School is currently linked to the University of Liverpool. For both courses you must use the institution code L41; the course code for Lancaster Medical School is A105. If you apply to both institutions this will take up two of your four choices.

Although Lancaster Medical School uses the same selection criteria as Liverpool applications are considered separately for the two degree programmes. Lancaster Medical School also uses a different interview process from Liverpool Medical School.

Leeds

Grades

GCSE

A reasonable range of good grades including at least 6 grade Bs including English and Maths, and either Dual Science or Chemistry and Biology.

AS/A Level

The typical offer we make is for three A levels at grades AAA and one of these is Chemistry. Chemistry can be offered with two non-science subjects as long as you have good grades at GCSE in either Biology or Double Science, but always check on the website prior to making an application.

We only look at three A level results. If you have more than three, we will consider the best three as long as they fulfil the criteria outlined above.

Work experience criteria

The School recognises that personal experience in a health and social care setting can make individuals more confident about choosing a career in medicine. Consequently, the School would like to know of any such experiences, what you learned and why it has helped make you more confident about your decision to study medicine. Normally you should be able to report some direct experience of either hospital or community medical practice. You should explain your work experience in your personal statement, and at your interview you'll have an opportunity to talk about your experience, your emotional response to it, what it has taught you and what you have gained from it.

If attempts to gain work experience have been unsuccessful, there should be some reference to this contained within the referee's statement.

A few examples of the types of work experience applicants have had follow but this is by no means an exhaustive list and in no particular order of importance: shadowing hospital doctors; shadowing members of the primary health care team; working in a pharmacy; shadowing radiographers, community nurses and physiotherapists.

Interview

Each (chosen) candidate will be asked a similar series of set questions. The questions are designed to explore the non-academic entry criteria that are stated in our admissions policy as well as test whether you have the skills and abilities required to succeed in a career in medicine.

Subject – personal statement/reference criteria

Your statement should include evidence of the following:
▸   insight into a career in medicine
▸   your academic record and achievements
▸   relevant life/work experiences
▸   responsibility

Check current online prospectus

> ▸ social and cultural awareness
> ▸ interests, activities and achievements.

We have produced a document with advice on writing your personal statement. This is available from our website.

We do read the personal reference given on the UCAS form when assessing applicants. However, we do not score the reference, merely noting if there are any issues that need to be considered further. Therefore, we would advise you do not use any of the reference section as an attempt to extend information on yourself that you did not mention in the personal statement section.

Please work with your referee when they are writing your reference to ensure they include as much appropriate information as possible and direct them to the guidance on the UCAS site (**www.ucas.com/advisors/online/references**).

Subject – how it is taught

Integrated

Test

UKCAT. There is no predetermined cut-off score. The scores will be considered when the assessors look at the whole of the application, which includes the personal statement, academic background and referee's statement.

Leicester

Grades

GCSE

We are interested in academic potential as well as previous achievements. We do not specify a minimum number of A* grades at GCSE. Please see our website selection criteria.

Candidates must have a minimum grade C in English Language, Mathematics and Double Science. It is important to remember, however, that many of our applicants have achieved a very high standard at GCSE.

Applicants must be predicted or have achieved AAA at A Level or 36 points (excluding core or bonus points) in the International Baccalaureate, in line with our standard offer.

GCSEs:

6 GCSE qualifications will be taken into account as below:
English language
Maths
Double Science (2)
Best two other subjects

OR

English language
Maths
Separate Sciences (up to 3)
Best other subject(s)

GCSE scoring will be as follows:

A* = 5, A = 4, B = 3, C = 2, D = 1

Achieved AS Results:

Additional points will be available for applicants who include AS results on their UCAS application, as follows:

An additional point for each A grade in the best three AS subjects including Chemistry, Biology and one other subject, up to the thirty points maximum total.

For example:

GCSE

English Language A = 4, Maths A* = 5, Double Science AA = 8, French A* = 5, Business Studies A* = 5

GCSE Total = 27

AS level

Chemistry A = 1, Biology A = 1, Other Subject A = 1

AS level Total = 3

Academic Grand Total = 30/30

Achieved A Level Results:

Additional points will be available for applicants who have already obtained A levels.

An additional point for each A* grade in the best three A level subjects, including Chemistry, up to the thirty points maximum total.

For example:

GCSE

English Language A = 4, Maths A* = 5, Double Science AA = 8, French A* = 5, Business Studies A* = 5

GCSE Total = 27

A level

Chemistry A* = 1, Other Subject A* = 1, Other Subject A = 0

A Level Total = 2

Academic Grand Total = 29/30

The AS results of candidates who have completed their A levels will not be taken into account in the assessment of academic attainment.

Following scoring of academic ability and UKCAT, candidates will be ranked. The lowest scoring candidates will not be considered further. The personal statement and reference of the remaining candidates will then be reviewed in order to assess personal qualities.

AS/A level

We require students to study four AS levels including Biology (or Human Biology) & Chemistry and to continue three of these subjects, including Chemistry, to A2 level. Our standard offer is based on performance at A2 level and is now AAA.

Work experience criteria

The way in which you can discover whether you have these qualities, and so demonstrate them to the selectors, is by undertaking significant work experience in the caring professions. This could include voluntary or paid work in a hospital, a residential home or other caring environment. However, we recognise the difficulties faced by some candidates in arranging this type of activity and the lack of such experience does not mean that an application will automatically be rejected.

These personal qualities are judged by consideration of the written material provided by the candidate from the referee's report on the UCAS form, and at interview.

Interview

Interviews will be held in a Multiple Mini Interview style for 2013 entry.

The various stations will assess the following:

▸ verbal communication

▸ written communication

▸ listening

▸ problem solving

▸ review of personal statement.

Subject – personal statement/reference criteria

The personal statement and reference may be used to generate a combined score out of 30, giving a total score for Personal Qualities. Where appropriate, the Personal Qualities score will be added to the academic and UKCAT score in order to determine the final ranking and selection for interview.

The following attributes will be considered:

▸ motivation

▸ commitment

▸ appreciation of challenges of a medical career

▸ work experience

▸ extracurricular activities

▸ contribution to school/college life

▸ contribution to wider community

▸ written communication skills

▸ support from teachers/staff

▸ confirmation of some aspects of personal statement in reference.

Subject – how it is taught

Integrated

Test

UKCAT will be scored according to the total, as follows:

3000+ = 30

2900+ = 29

2800+ = 28

2700+ = 27

Etc.

Liverpool

Grades

GCSE

GCSEs in nine separate subject areas at a minimum of grade C: attained by the end of Year 11 and at least a score of fifteen points or better (where A*/A = 2; B = 1) from the nine and including: Core & Additional Science (or Biology, Chemistry and Physics), English Language and Mathematics (all at least grade B). Preference will be given to applicants with a higher GCSE score.

AS/A level

A levels in three subjects taken at one sitting after two years of study (plus a 4th subject to at least AS level): at a minimum of AAA(b) Chemistry and Biology are subject requirements at A2 level. Only one of Maths or Further Maths will be considered. The Extended Project qualification may be acceptable at grade B in place of the AS level qualification in some instances.

Applications from candidates re-sitting advance level examinations may be considered if the applicant otherwise meets the GCSE criteria (as above). Applicants must acknowledge and reflect on their need to re-sit in the personal statement.

Work experience criteria

No formal work experience is specified but applicants will need to address our non-academic criteria and include the demonstration of health care career awareness/insight, a caring contribution to the local community and a critical, coherent and informative approach to communication.

Evidence of appropriate experience, aptitude, and communication:

▶ Candidates must demonstrate suitable evidence of:

▶ health care career awareness/insight and

▶ a caring contribution to the local community and

▶ a critical, coherent, and informative approach to written communication.

Interview

Applicants are invited to an approximately fifteen minute, semi-structured interview with two people drawn from a panel of trained interviewers, including academic members of the university staff, NHS clinicians, local GPs and members of local NHS trusts.

The criteria used to assess the interview are application of knowledge of the Liverpool medical programme and its curriculum, medical ethics and team work, together with the non-academic criteria as previously stated

Subject – personal statement/reference criteria

Applicants demonstrating the most academic potential are then assessed against our non-academic criteria, which include health care career awareness and insight, caring for the local community and a critical, coherent and informative approach to written communication. Those who most ably demonstrate that they fulfil these criteria when compared on a competitive basis with other applicants are invited to interview. The information available in the academic reference is also assessed and a reference should aim to be as informative as possible and personalised to emphasise the strengths and personal qualities of the applicant it supports.

Subject – how is it taught

Problem-based learning

Test

Neither the UKCAT nor any other national university entrance test is used in selection for the Liverpool Medical Programmes.

Manchester

Grades

GCSE

At least seven subjects are required at grade C or above; at least five must be at A or A*. English Language and Mathematics are required at GCSE minimum grade B. All applicants are expected to adhere to these GCSE requirements. If you are re-sitting any GCSE subjects, you must explain the extenuating circumstances that prompted this.

Physics and Biology are required either at AS or at GCSE at minimum grade C. (Chemistry is essential at A2.) If Dual Award Science or Core and Additional Science are offered, the minimum required is BB. In Grade A requirements, the School do not currently accept Applied ICT, Applied Business or short courses.

AS/A/Level

The School's normal A level offer after successful interview would be grades AAA, with exams taken at the same sitting after no more than two years of study.

Chemistry plus one from Biology or Human Biology, Physics, Mathematics or Further Mathematics plus one further subject (not Critical Thinking or General Studies; Further Mathematics not accepted alongside Mathematics; we do not accept Applied A levels for either the 5-year or 6-year programme).

Predicted A2 grades of AAA required.

We expect at least four subjects at AS level. We are aware that the curriculum for some schools will only allow three AS subjects to be taken. These students will not be disadvantaged if written confirmation of this policy is provided by the school.

Work experience criteria, subject – personal statement/reference criteria

Amount of work experience in a caring role

This does not necessarily mean medically related work experience, such as shadowing a GP or consultant. Such experience can be difficult to obtain for students under the age of 18. However, we are interested in caring experience, which may or may not be medically related. Tell us how you got involved in such work, how long you have been doing it, how much time you spend each week and, most importantly, what you have gained from it.

In the second stage of the process trained selectors will check the personal statement and reference for:

- insight and reflection on a medical career
- motivation towards a medical career
- work experience in a caring role
- interests/hobbies and linking these with ability to cope with stress
- evidence of teamwork, leadership skills and communication skills.

Any applications rejected formally after the second screening will have been re-assessed independently by a senior member of the admissions team.

Applicants should be aware that information provided in the personal statement may be used as the basis for further discussion during any subsequent interview.

A 'character reference' is not sufficient. We do, however, want to know what the writer of the reference thinks about you as a whole person, not merely about your academic achievements and potential.

Interview

The aim of the interview is to explore the non-academic criteria (see above) as well as to encourage applicants to talk naturally about themselves, their studies and their experiences, and to demonstrate that they have the interpersonal skills to be able to communicate effectively and show that they are well-rounded individuals. In this way they can show that they meet the academic and non-academic attributes required of a prospective doctor.

The interview process is in two parts:

30 minute group task with up to 9 candidates
One-to-one interviews of 8 minutes each at three separate stations:
Ability to communicate
Communication skills are essential to the practice of almost all aspects of medicine. We expect candidates to be able to express their ideas clearly and coherently and to be able to follow a reasoned argument. Candidates who give spontaneous yet well-thought-out answers to questions are more likely to impress the interviewers than those who give obviously rehearsed and 'coached' responses.

Why do you want to be a doctor?

This is an obvious but vital question. It is also the question to which candidates most frequently reply with a coached and practised answer. We will seek specific evidence of the experiences that have influenced your decision to study medicine.

Previous caring experience

Your experiences in a caring role will be of great interest. These need not be in a traditional mainstream medical environment. The interview is an opportunity for candidates to relate not only to the facts and details of their experiences, but also their emotional responses to them and what they have gained from them.

Matters of a medical interest

Candidates will not be expected to have detailed knowledge of medical processes. However, the interviewers will expect you to have an intelligent layperson's view on contemporary aspects of medicine, particularly those of current media interest.

Ethical and other issues

Ethical issues may be raised by the interviewers, but only to assess your ability to coherently summarise the issues at stake. Candidates should be reassured that neither the interviewers nor the Medical School will take a position on any ethical issue. It is not the candidate's ethical views that the interviewers may be interested in, but how coherently the candidate expresses the ethical dilemmas facing medical practitioners. Candidates will not be asked questions in any of the following areas: gender, sexuality, marital or parental status, race, religion, social background.

What will the interview involve?

The interview process held in Manchester is in two parts:

▸ The first thirty minutes will be spent with other applicants in a group task discussing a medical scenario. The first ten minutes will be allocated to individual thought; the remaining time will be spent trying to reach consensus within the group. Three interviewers will observe the process. We do not expect you to have any more than a layperson's general knowledge of the medical issues. The intention is to get you to relax and for us to be able to assess your team working skills.

▸ In the second thirty minutes you will have one-to-one interviews at three separate stations. At one station you will be asked to reflect on the group discussion. At the second, the interviewer will have a copy of your personal statement and may discuss any relevant point from your personal statement. The third station will be devoted to a discussion of issues from a wider nature in the fields of medicine. The three stations may not appear in this order.

Subject – how it is taught

Problem-based learning

Test

To help identify talented students from all backgrounds, UKCAT scores from UK candidates who come from similar educational and socio-demographic backgrounds are considered against one another. This is done by using supplemental information provided by publicly available datasets (see **www.manchester.ac.uk/contextualdata**). Equal proportions of top scoring applicants from each group are then selected for interview.

The following tables give the range of UKCAT scores for applicants who were invited to interview last year.

These are intended as a guide only; as we do not receive the UKCAT results prior to application, we cannot predict the score needed to obtain an interview.

UKCAT scores of applicants invited for interview for A106:

UKCAT scores of applicants invited for interview for A106 admissions cycle	Applicants with a WP Plus Flag (i.e., those who meet both geo-demographic and educational indicators, and /or those who have been in care for more than three months)	Applicants with a WP Flag or no contextual flags
2012/13	2560 and above	2650 and above
2011/12	2490 and above	2590 and above
2010/11	2460 and above	2610 and above

Do not use this information as a final reference source! Always check current online prospectuses as this information may not fully represent the holistic scoring process used, and could be out of date very quickly. This chapter is a one-stop shop, giving advisors and applicants a realistic idea of the range of criteria that needs to be met.

Newcastle (and Durham)

Grades

GCSE/AS/A levels

Applicants wishing to be considered with A levels are required to achieve AAA. Subjects should include Chemistry or Biology at A or AS level. If only one of Biology and/or Chemistry is offered at A or AS level, the other should be offered at GCSE grade A (or Dual Award Science grade A). We do not accept General Studies or Critical Thinking as an A level entry qualification. We would normally expect applicants to sit all three A levels in the same academic year.

Work experience criteria

Assessed at interview – see interview notes

Interview, subject – personal statement/reference criteria

Newcastle Interview

The following are the interview processes used at Newcastle University. These may differ slightly to those used at Durham University, Queen's Campus, Stockton.

The interview will be conducted by two selectors and will last approximately twenty-five minutes. At the conclusion of the interview each selector will grade the candidate's performance and complete an assessment form. These grades are used as the basis for the decision-making process for actual offers. Selectors will not convey their grades to the candidates at the time of the interview or at any time thereafter.

At interview applicants to the standard five year programme (A100) will be assessed and graded under five main categories:

▸ Choice of Newcastle.

▸ Reflection on commitment to care and role of a doctor. This will cover commitment to care of others, insight into a career and the role of a doctor, understanding the NHS and ethical issues.

▸ Reflection on personal attributes. This will cover learning styles, communication skills, fluency and ability to deal with questions, ability to explain a specific concept, non-academic and personal interests (ability to describe personal interests and expand on those described), personal attributes (strengths/weaknesses, self-motivation, leadership, teamwork and coping with stress).

▸ Verification of personal statement. Ability to verify their personal statement, drawing on examples therein and expanding on them.

▸ Overall performance at interview.

The selectors will assess the overall performance of the applicant and award an overall score.

Your personal statement, reference and contribution at interview are the sources from which the selectors will make their judgement.

Durham Interview

All those regarded as being suitable potential entrants are invited to attend an interview at Queen's Campus, Stockton with two trained selectors, who will be health professionals, academic members of staff and/or members of the community. The interview focuses on exploring important personal qualities.

Subject – how it is taught

Integrated

Test

For the A100 programme Newcastle and Durham use the same UKCAT threshold to identify applicants for interview.

The UKCAT threshold may differ in each admissions cycle as it is dependent on the scores achieved by those applicants who apply to our medical school in the current cycle. Therefore information on what the threshold is is not available to prospective students.

Norwich University of East Anglia

Grades

GCSE

All applicants must have a minimum of six GCSE (or equivalent) passes at grade A or above to include English, Maths and two Science subjects. GCSE short courses are not accepted.

AS/A levels

AAA to include Biology/Human Biology and one other science plus AS level grade B in a fourth subject.

Second science subject from Chemistry, Physics, Mathematics or Further Mathematics.

NB: Combinations of Mathematics and Further Mathematics are not accepted at A2/AS level. We are looking for four separate subjects, three at full A level and one at AS as a minimum. We consider Mathematics and Further Mathematics to be one subject area.

General Studies and Critical Thinking are not accepted at A2 or AS level.

Norwich Medical School will consider A level re-sits if grades BBB were obtained at the first sitting.

Candidates who are wishing to re-sit one subject only will be required to have a predicted A*.

Candidates re-sitting two A level subjects are required to have predicted grades of A*A.

Candidates re-sitting three A level subjects are required to have predicted grades of A*AA.

All candidates should have a fourth AS or A level at grade B.

Re-sit AS modules. Your full A level (AS and A2) should be completed within a two-year period. This may include re-sitting modules. Any additional study outside of this period will be subject to our re-sit policy.

Check current online prospectus

Work experience criteria

We email applicants directly who have been invited to interview. If you are invited to interview you are required to bring with you a completed work experience form. This asks you to provide details of two experiences that have most informed your decision to study Medicine (for example, but not limited to: voluntary work, 'shadowing' a health care professional, paid employment, or personal experience caring for others). Please include contact details of someone who can verify your experiences, and bring the completed form to your interview. You should be prepared to discuss your experiences at the interview.

Interview

Each interview lasts approximately fifty minutes. Candidates will be invited to take part in an OSCE (Objective Structured Clinical Examination) style interview, also known as a Multiple Mini Interview. When candidates enter the interview section, they will find a series of booths, known as 'stations'. There will be seven stations to circulate through, spending approximately five minutes at each station. Further details will be provided to each candidate at the time they are invited to interview.

Subject – personal statement criteria

Successful applicants will have demonstrated, among other things, an understanding of health care and the role and responsibilities of a doctor, evidence of suitability to join the profession and good communication and organisational skills.

Subject – type of degree

We offer a PBL (Problem Based Learning) integrated curriculum supported by a comprehensive programme of lectures and seminars, with early and regular patient-centred teaching in both primary and secondary care starting in week two of the course.

Test

We have not set a minimum cut-off score for the UKCAT test. We will consider scores from the test within the academic screening processes in the School. While a high UKCAT score could be advantageous a low score will not automatically disqualify a candidate from consideration. If the rest of the application is strong then the applicant could still be short-listed for interview with a lower UKCAT test score.

Nottingham

Grades

GCSE/A level/AS level

AAA–A in Chemistry and Biology at A level; third A level at grade A in any subject except general studies and critical thinking; we do not have a preference for the third subject. Once A levels have been certificated, we will not accept any module re-sits.

At least six GCSEs at grade A including Chemistry, Physics and Biology or Double Science; GCSE grade B in English and Maths. If you didn't achieve an A grade in Physics at GCSE, you can compensate this by taking the subject to AS and achieving an A grade. This only applies to Physics.

AS levels – we don't ask for particular grades at AS level. We will look at them to ensure that either an A or B was achieved in the subjects being taken further to A level.

Work experience criteria

Medical applicants are expected to have undergone some form of medical work experience to enable them to understand the profession they are entering.

Keeping a reflective diary will enable you to write down your experiences and what you have learned from them. Keeping this up to date at the end of each work experience session will enable you to remember your experiences and will provide you with preparation material for when you write your personal statement and before you attend an interview.

Work experience should include: speaking to doctors and, where possible, observing doctors. You may have the opportunity to watch doctors perform operations, however it would be more beneficial for you to focus more on the following:

▸ Consider the skills doctors need to be able to carry out their duties. Then, when observing doctors, observe how they use the skills. The use of these skills could differ depending on their medical specialty, for example a GP or a surgeon.

▸ Observe their interaction with other health care professionals.

▸ If you are unable to observe a doctor, then ask a doctor what skills they consider important for their specialty.

▸ Ask doctors what they like about their profession and specialty and what they dislike. Try to ask more than one doctor these questions as their likes and dislikes may differ.

Experience in a more caring setting – a hospice or care home or similar. This will allow you to observe more long-term interactions between carers and patients and the skills required in this particular role. Consider what it would be like to be in the patient's position and think about their requirements and needs and how these may be met by carers.

Interview

You must first meet our minimum academic requirements as outlined in the Qualifications section above. We then score certain areas of your application as explained below:

We score:

1 Highest eight GCSEs including the sciences (the three separate sciences or the science double award), maths and English language, A* and A grades.

2 Personal and referees statements.

3 Online questionnaire – information on how to complete this is given to you once the application deadline of 15 October has passed.

4 UKCAT – the scores achieved for each of the four cognitive components are internally scored.

The above scores are totalled and those with the highest total scores are invited for interview. Therefore, if you don't feel you have done well on one of the above areas you may still achieve a total score that will be sufficient for interview.

Our interviews are traditional in format. The questions during the interview will focus on the following: motivation, empathy and communication skills.

Familiarise yourself with the interview style we use and the themes that will be addressed at interview.

Review the following: your application and your personal statement; work experience and reflective diary accounts; the type of medicine course at Nottingham; any medically related items that have appeared in the media over the past few months.

Subject – personal statement criteria

This is your opportunity to tell us about yourself, the medical insight you have gained from your work experience and other achievements and hobbies.

We want to understand: what has motivated you to want a career in medicine, the work experience you have carried out and what you have learned from it, non-academic achievements and hobbies and activities you are undertaking at school

Subject – how it is taught

Integrated

Test

UKCAT – We don't have a threshold score for UKCAT.

Oxford

GCSE

You would be expected to hold a broad range of GCSEs, in both sciences and arts subjects. You should have top results – that is mostly A*s and As – for your application to be competitive. On average, our applicants hold about 70% of GCSEs grades at A* – although successful applicants may have a lower or higher proportion of A*s than this.

A/ AS level

3 A levels, including:

▸ Chemistry (compulsory) *and*

▸ at least one from Biology, Physics and Mathematics.

The typical conditional offer is A*AA (taken in one academic year).

AS level grades are not used formally in our ranking process. It would be usual for applicants to have achieved A grades in AS subjects particularly relevant for Medicine, such as Chemistry, but we take great care to assess each applicant as an individual (any personal or school circumstances that may have affected examination performance will be recognised). We are looking for individuals with capability to do well at a course that is demanding both in breadth and depth: An applicant who is struggling to reach the standard of an A grade at AS level may not be well-suited to it.

Work experience criteria

Our tutors select students using the selection criteria (below). All applicants are free to make reference to skills or experience acquired in any context to date when trying to address our selection criteria: Sometimes applicants refer to voluntary work and other extra-curricular activity, but many forms of evidence can help demonstrate to tutors that an applicant has tried to make an informed decision regarding his/her own suitability to study Medicine.

While some work experience in hospitals is theoretically desirable, we do appreciate that it can be very difficult to arrange and we therefore have no requirement for it. Any form of voluntary work would be beneficial in the context of applying for Medicine (such as helping out in a hospital, at an old people's home, St John's Ambulance, or work with a charity or overseas agency).

Interview, subject – personal statement criteria

Personal characteristics: suitability for medicine:

▸ empathy: ability and willingness to imagine the feelings of others and understand the reasons for the views of others

▸ motivation: a reasonably well-informed and strong desire to practise medicine

▸ communication: ability to make knowledge and ideas clear using language appropriate to the audience

▸ honesty and integrity

▸ ethical awareness

▸ ability to work with others

▸ capacity for sustained and intense work.

Academic potential

▸ Problem-solving: critical thinking, analytical approach

▸ Intellectual curiosity: keenness to understand the reason for observations, depth, tendency to look for meaning, enthusiasm and curiosity in science

▸ Communication skills: willingness and ability to express clearly and effectively, ability to listen, compatibility with tutorial format

Two or three interviews – that may be individual or panel.

Subject – how it is taught

Traditional

Test

How well you need to do in BMAT will be entirely dependent on how well every other applicant does, and how well you have done in GCSEs (if you have taken them). A slightly weaker performance at GCSE may be compensated for by a very good BMAT score, and vice-versa. However, to offer a rough guide, we would suggest that the typical average applicant should be working towards a six (a seven is still fairly rare) in sections one or two; do note that sections one and two receive greater weighting (40% each) than section three (20%). Applicants should undertake thorough preparation for BMAT – they should practice taking the test to familiarise themselves with the format of it and increase their chances of obtaining a high score.

Plymouth

Grades

GCSE

Applicants need to achieve seven GCSE passes at grades A–C, which must include English Language, Mathematics and either GCSE Single and Additional Science or GCSE Biology and Chemistry.

Check current online prospectus

Check current online prospectus

AS/A levels

The typical offer is A*AA – AAA at GCE A level, which must include Chemistry and either Biology or Physics. A fourth subject must be achieved at a minimum of grade C at AS level. If Biology is not offered at A level, it must be achieved at a minimum of grade C at AS level. General Studies at A/AS level is not included within any offer.

Work experience criteria, interview

The interview is structured and formal to make sure every student is asked the same questions and receives the same prompts. It's not a test of your scientific knowledge but aims to explore your attitudes, outlook and way of thinking. The interview is a structured process of approximately twenty minutes, using a predetermined scoring system. This is to help ensure that candidates receive as close to an identical experience as possible. On each interview day candidates will attend an introductory talk giving further details about the interview process prior to completing pre-interview exercises.

Home/EU fee-paying interviewees will be asked to complete the following two pre-interview exercises, for which they have half an hour:

▶ complete a written questionnaire, which aims to investigate a candidate's commitment and motivation to study medicine or dentistry

▶ consider three scenarios, which centre upon contemporary ethical issues related to medicine or dentistry, and select one as the basis for their interview.

If you're selected for interview for the BMBS programme you need to show us you have the following essential qualities to become a doctor of tomorrow:

▶ integrity

▶ veracity and honesty

▶ flexibility

▶ motivation and commitment

▶ pro-social attitudes e.g., students who show empathy and who are non-judgmental

▶ communication skills, including listening

▶ potential for leadership

▶ students who show insight into what it is to be a doctor

▶ the ability to be a team player

▶ the ability to deal with stress appropriately

▶ problem solving skills

▶ students who know their limitations, their strengths and weaknesses

▶ reflectiveness

▶ students who demonstrate a suitable approach to life and people.

Subject – personal statement criteria

None stated

Type of degree

Structured small group learning (PBL)

Test

PU PSMD uses the UK Clinical Aptitude Test (UKCAT) in order to make more informed choices from among the many applicants who apply with predicted grades for a place on the BMBS programme. UKCAT test results are used alongside the academic information provided on the UCAS form in order to select candidates for interview.

Queen's University Belfast

Grades (stage 1)

GCSE

For Y14 (year 13) applicants the best nine GCSEs will be considered with 4 marks for an A star and three for an A. Maximum 36 points.

Mathematics and Physics (or Double Award Science) are required if not offered at AS or A level.

GCSE Short Courses attract 2 points for an A* and 1.5 for an A grade. Two Short Courses will count as one GCSE in calculation of the best nine subjects. Care is taken to ensure that applicants are awarded the maximum points possible.

AS/A level

AAAa

Three A levels are required to include GCE Chemistry + at least one from Biology, Physics and Maths. A maximum of one VCE/Applied subject at either A level or AS level (not both) will be counted. If Biology is not offered at GCE A level, it is required at GCE AS grade B or better. Mathematics and Further Mathematics cannot be counted together at A level but one may be counted at A level and the other at AS level.

Module repeats within the normal two-year period between GCSE and A level do not place applicants at any disadvantage. An A level taken a year early would also be counted.

Interview (stage 2)

Multiple Mini Interviews

Applicants selected for stage two of the admissions process will be asked to attend a nine station Multiple Mini Interview (MMI) to determine non-cognitive performance. MMIs are being used to test non-cognitive competence and the applicant's personal statement is considered within this process.

These interviews have been designed to test the following, which have been identified by both patients and academic staff as key non-cognitive competencies for medicine:

▸ empathy
▸ problem-solving
▸ moral reasoning
▸ communication skills.

Short videos on website

Sample interview station 1

You the candidate are asked to assume you are a first year medical student and that on your way home from class you reach a bus stop. At the bus stop a class mate is sitting there looking glum, obviously upset. You don't know their name. Demonstrate how you would approach this situation. Your class mate will be waiting at the bus stop when you enter the station.

This station has been designed to test the candidate's ability to communicate and to demonstrate empathy.

The format of this example is a semi-structured interview with an examiner.

Non-cognitive competencies being assessed:

▸ problem solving

▸ ethical reasoning

▸ communication.

Sample Interview Station 2

Instruction to the candidate:

Your mother rings you and asks you to come round and help with a major family decision. Her 70 year old father has been diagnosed with a condition that will kill him sometime in the next five years. He can have a procedure that will correct the disease and not leave him with any long-term problems, but the procedure has a 10% mortality rate. He wants to have the procedure but your mother is not in favour of it. How would you help mediate this issue?

Aim of the question (seen by the interviewer only) to find out if the candidate:

▸ demonstrates sensitivity to the needs of others

▸ understands the right of the patient to be fully involved in decisions about their care

▸ can think of ways to help resolve a situation when emotional issues may cloud one's judgement

▸ understands the limit of their own knowledge and experience.

Work experience, subject – personal statement/reference criteria (stage 1)

The following general factors are taken into account when considering applications:

(i) Candidates are expected to state explicitly that Medicine is their career choice. (Please note that an applicant cannot normally be considered for both Medicine and dentistry). There should be evidence of commitment and motivation in the personal statement. This should include evidence of what the candidate has done to find out about Medicine as a career. This can be demonstrated in a number of ways including: opportunities for observational experience in a clinical setting, attending medical careers conferences or undertaking voluntary work in a care setting. Participation in activities within or outside school demonstrating transferable skills such as leadership, empathy, teamwork and communication skills is also considered.

(ii) Satisfactory support from the academic referee, particularly relating to the applicant's character, suitability for the course, communication skills and initiative.

Type of degree

Integrated

Tests (stage 1)

All applicants will take the UKCAT* in the year of entry and their overall score will attract up to six points; see Table 1 below. This score will be added to their knowledge-based mark and all applicants ranked. The top circa 500 applicants will then be considered under stage 2 of the selection process, which will be a nine station multiple mini interview (MMI) to determine non-cognitive performance. MMIs are being used to test non-cognitive competence and the applicant's personal statement is considered within this process.

Table 1: Total UKCAT Banding Scores for Applicants Applying for Medicine at Queen's University Belfast in 2012

Band score	Scoring range
0	1200–1899
1	1900–2099
2	2100–2299
3	2300–2499
4	2500–2699
5	2700–2899
6	2900–3600

Final decisions about whether or not to make an offer will be made on the basis of interview ranking alone (i.e. stage 2 results) and not in combination with other factors.

Sheffield

Grades

GCSE

You must have GCSE passes, or their equivalent, at grade C or above in English, Mathematics and the Sciences (that may be dual awards). You should have at least six A grades in GCSE subjects.

AS/A level

You should study four AS levels. The subjects studied must include Chemistry and another science (Maths, Physics, Biology or Psychology). You should aim to achieve grades of at least ABBB in these subjects.

Our offer for subjects taken at A level is AAA to include Chemistry and another science (Maths, Physics, Biology or Psychology). It is expected that these examinations are taken in the same sitting as we are unable to consider re-sits or examinations taken early. Please note that in some cases we may not be able to consider a Modern Language as a third A level. Please contact the department for further information.

On UCAS Apply, *all* A level candidates *must* declare their individual module UMS scores in the box marked 'Other' adjacent to the module information. UMS scores must be recorded as actual score achieved/maximum score possible for the module (numerator/denominator for each module taken). Candidates with certificated A1/AS level grades should enter their UMS score for each module as above, and their grade for the A1/AS level overall.

Check current online prospectus

Work experience criteria

A good personal statement will include information on your relevant work experience. Medical schools expect applicants to have a range of work experience for two reasons. First, this demonstrates that you have a realistic insight into the profession – you are after all committing to a lifetime career when you apply to study Medicine. It is important that you have an understanding of the complex nature of a doctor's role, as well as being aware of the highs and lows of the profession.

Work experience is also important in enabling you to develop (and to demonstrate that you have) the relevant skills and qualities that are essential to becoming a good doctor. A few examples are listed below.

▶   communication skills

▶   a sense of service to the community

▶   a sense of responsibility

▶   self-insight

▶   enthusiasm

▶   perseverance

▶   ability to overcome setbacks

▶   ability to work independently

▶   experience of working with diverse groups.

We recognise that it is not always possible for students to obtain work placements in a medical environment given the limited availability of volunteer placements in hospitals and similar clinical settings. However, in addition to shadowing a GP or other medical practitioner, there are many other areas related to medicine in which you can gain experience. Some examples of these are listed below:

▶   paid or voluntary work experience in a residential care home, hospice or similar.

▶   working in a youth centre or working with young children.

▶   participating in community volunteering schemes.

▶   working with a diverse range of people (whether on a paid or voluntary basis).

Participatory work experience (not simply observing, but a 'hands-on' role) is extremely valuable. Many applicants arrange to undertake paid or voluntary work as a health care assistant. Whatever work experience you have, it is important that you reflect effectively on this in your personal statement.

Your personal statement should communicate not only what meaningful activities you have undertaken, but also what you have learned from these experiences, for example, how they have changed reinforced your views. Discussing a highlight or poor experience is welcomed. We are not looking for a rota of the duties your job or project involved! Your personal statement should highlight how this insight into health care will enable you to become a good medical practitioner in the future.

Interview

Once your application has been given a score for your academic achievements and your personal qualities we will look at the combination of the two scores you have been given. Candidates with the highest grades for their academic achievements and personal qualities will be invited for interview.

The interview panel normally consists of three interviewers. These are drawn from medically qualified senior members of staff, biomedical scientists, junior hospital doctors, senior nurses, senior medical students and lay people. The questioning at interview is based around the following criteria:

▸ knowledge of and interest in study in Sheffield

▸ motivation for Medicine

▸ evidence of commitment for caring

▸ depth and width of interests (achievements in specific fields)

▸ communication skills

▸ understanding the nature of Medicine

▸ medical work experience.

The interview panel will have a copy of your UCAS application. While you will not be questioned on every aspect in your personal statement you can expect the panel to ask you about topics or areas that you have mentioned. You can also prepare by keeping up to date with recent medical breakthroughs, topical controversies, ethical issues and NHS politics.

Of course your appearance at interview is important. You should dress appropriately and in a professional manner.

Subject – personal statement/reference criteria

When the assessors read your personal statement they are looking for:

▸ motivation for medicine

▸ evidence of commitment for caring

▸ work experience

▸ understanding the nature of medicine

▸ breadth and depth of interests, and linking these with ability to cope with stress

▸ evidence of team work, leadership skills, communication skills and acceptance of responsibility.

On the basis of your personal statement and the reference the assessors will give you an overall score for your personal qualities.

Personal qualities that the University of Sheffield are interested in are listed alphabetically, and in no particular order of importance, in the box. These qualities include characters, talents and abilities. This list is not intended to be exhaustive and we recognise that there are many other qualities that may benefit the future professional. We consider it unlikely that any individual possesses every one of these, and other desirable qualities, and do NOT advise candidates to treat them as a checklist.

We wish to review the personal and teacher statements for evidence of such qualities, in order to build a personal profile of the candidate, and we will further explore these areas at interview. It is important to highlight evidence rather than to make unsupported statements or engage in a form of false modesty. It should also be clear that truth-telling is a vital component of professional behaviour, and we will view any untruth or significant exaggeration very seriously.

Personal qualities might include (alphabetically):

Concern for others, conscientiousness, courage, determination, diligence, flexibility, humility, initiative, interpersonal skills, leadership, long-term commitment, orderly, organisation, public performance, responsibility, self-directed study skills, time management and Trustworthiness.

Subject – how it is taught

Integrated

Test

UKCAT

All applicants will be expected to have taken the UKCAT examination. The University of Sheffield considers that the evidence for using UKCAT as the primary determinant in medical school admission is not strong. Therefore, all applicants scoring above 2400 (600 average, approximately fiftieth percentile) in the UKCAT, who meet the other academic criteria, will be considered.

Southampton

Grades

GCSE

A minimum of seven GCSEs at grades A*, A or B, including Mathematics, English and Double Award Science (or equivalent).

AS/A level

AAA, including Chemistry (alternatively, AS level Chemistry and Biology/Human Biology can be offered at grade A in addition to grades AAA at A level). General Studies is not accepted. Subjects with material that overlaps (e.g. Biology/Sports Studies, Maths/Further Maths) may not be accepted in combination at A level.

Work experience criteria

You need to show you have learned from experiences of interacting with people in health or social care settings – this could be helping to look after an ill family member or friend or could be voluntary/paid work or work shadowing. It can be difficult to obtain experience in a hospital setting so you could work/volunteer in a nursing home, homeless shelter or local hospice or could work with people with special needs or a youth group.

Interview

No interview

Subject – personal statement/reference criteria

The selectors will look at your UCAS personal statement and reference for evidence of non-academic criteria.

You will be asked to demonstrate that you:

▸ are self-motivated and have initiative

▸ are literate and articulate

▸ are able to interact successfully with others

▸ have learned from your experiences of interacting with people in health or social care settings – this may draw on what you have learned from your own life experiences (e.g. friends and family), or more formalised activity (e.g. paid or voluntary work, or work shadowing).

Check current online prospectus

Subject – how it is taught

Integrated

Test

UKCAT

From 2013 entry, applicants to A100 programmes must score 2500 or above in the UKCAT exam in order for their application to be considered further.

St Andrews

Grades

GCSE/AS/A level

▸ AAA (Advanced levels) including Chemistry and one other of Biology, Mathematics or Physics.

▸ If Biology, Mathematics and English are not offered at Advanced (A2) or AS Level, each must normally have been passed at GCSE grade B or better. Dual award Science is not acceptable in lieu of GCSE Biology.

▸ Human Biology may replace Biology.

▸ General Studies and Critical Thinking are not considered.

▸ Advanced levels must be studied over a two-year period and completed in Year 13.

▸ Only one of Mathematics or Further Mathematics will be considered for the three subjects required at Advanced level.

From experience of applications in previous years it would appear that to be competitive, applicants with A levels require a minimum of eight A grades at GCSE (to include Maths and Sciences) and predictions of A*AA at A level.

Work experience criteria

Applicants should try to gain as wide an experience as possible in a caring or health environment. This does not have to be in a hospital (that can be difficult to obtain) but a nursing home, local hospice, shelter for the homeless, working with people with disabilities or special needs, or working with a youth group, would all be useful experience.

Interview

The interview itself is a formal though friendly process and lasts twenty minutes. The interview panel comprises two (occasionally three) interviewers.

The interview panel, in addition to forming an overall impression of the student, will be assessing in particular the following areas:

Ability to communicate

Communication skills are essential to the practice of almost all aspects of medicine. We expect candidates to be able to express their ideas clearly and coherently and to be able to follow a reasoned argument. Just before your interview you will be asked to read a short article on a medically related topic. This will only take about ten minutes. The interview panel will then ask you questions about the article. They will be assessing your comprehension and ability to summarise as well as communication skills.

The St Andrews course

The panel will expect the candidate to have a general understanding of our course – details of which can be obtained from our website. In particular, we expect candidates to be aware of the way in which we deliver the Medical programme and to have an opinion on its appeal to them, its advantages and limitations.

Previous experience

The interview panel will be interested in how you have prepared yourself for entering into a medical career. They will be keen to know what you have gained from work experience in a medical or 'caring' environment or indeed some other environment that you feel has been relevant in preparing you for a career in medicine.

After interviews applicants are ranked on the basis of all four areas of assessment: academic performance, personal statement and reference, UKCAT score and interview score.

Each of the four areas of assessment is given a different weighting:

- academic performance: 50%
- UKCAT: 15%
- personal statement and reference: 15%
- interview: 20%.

Offers are then made from the top of the ranking in relation to the number of places available.

Subject – personal statement criteria

We will want you to show evidence of commitment to helping others, the ways in which you have contributed to your school/college/community activities and to demonstrate a wide range of interests and personal achievements.

Explain what your interests and hobbies are and why you enjoy them and indicate how long you have pursued them. Tell us about any awards you have won and explain what skills you have gained rather than simply listing your activities. It is essential that you are able to communicate, empathise and work well with others.

Successful applicants will be able to show evidence of the following:

- personal qualities such as empathy, good communication and listening skills, leadership skills and the ability to work in a team
- a well-informed understanding of what a career in medicine involves
- commitment to medicine by organising work experience or shadowing; working with ill, disabled, or disadvantaged people, preferably in health care settings
- commitment to academic study, staying power, perseverance and intellectual potential
- non-academic achievement: positions of responsibility, organisational ability, interests and hobbies, cultural and sporting activities and achievements, social involvement

It is important that the choice to enter medicine is made with insight into where it might lead, the expectations of others, the role of life-long learning, and with awareness that the course is a training for professional practice.

Subject – how it is taught

Traditional

Test

At St Andrews we use the UKCAT in two ways:

First we set a cut off for the overall UKCAT score and applicants obtaining a score below that will not be considered for interview or a medical place. The cut-off level depends on the number of strong applicants each year and the number of interview places available. A cut-off score for each admissions cycle will be decided upon once all applications have been assessed.

Second, at St Andrews the UKCAT score will be used as part of an applicant's overall ranking following interview. The UKCAT score will be worth 15% of an overall admissions score. That percentage will be generated by a points system whereby applicant scores will be ranked and divided into bandings with points allocated per banding. In order to be competitive and obtain an offer, a high score would be advantageous. The average global UKCAT score for those who obtained an offer for 2012 entry was 2700.

St Georges University of London (SGUL)

Grades

GCSE

An average of A in the top 8 subjects, which must include English Language (minimum grade B), Maths and the Sciences (dual award or three separate sciences). This equates to 416 points Key Stage 4 average points score per pupil – best 8.

*Will only accept a complete set of scores from one sitting.

AS/A level

AAA at A level with a grade B in a fourth subject at AS Level. This must include both Chemistry and Biology either both to A level or one to A level and the other to AS level.

General Studies and Key Skills are not accepted.

A levels must be completed within two years; re-sits will not be considered.

If you are offering grades lower than AAA with a grade B in your fourth AS, your application will be considered if this achievement is 60 per cent higher than the average performance of your school/college.* Candidates with predicted grades lower than BBC will not be considered and Chemistry and Biology must be awarded at grade B.

*You can find your school average at the DFE School Performance Tables.

You must still meet the GCSE requirement of an average of A in the top eight subjects.

N.B: Grades are considered in conjunction with UKCAT score (see below).

Work experience criteria

Voluntary or work experience in a medical- or health-related field will be assessed at interview as well as and an ability to demonstrate a broad awareness of the scope of medicine.

Visit The Taste of Medicine (Experience It) website for further information about work experience.

Also when invited to the MMI day you will also be asked to complete a form in advance detailing your work experience that you must bring on the day.

Interview

We have introduced the Multi-Mini Interview (MMI) as part of selection. MMIs are short, focused interactions from which we are able to gain valuable insights into an applicant's potential. MMIs combine traditional style questions with task-based activities. This provides a high level of interaction and the opportunity to demonstrate more than just a taught knowledge of the field of medicine. Visit Taste of Medicine (Scrubbing Up) website to gain further insight into how to prepare for your interview.

Example MMI tasks

As well as traditional questions, some stations will involve task-based scenarios. Here is an example of the sorts of tasks you could be set:

▸ Pack a suitcase for a trip, where the case can only contain half of the items available.

▸ Travelling on the London Underground, one of your friends has become separated from the group – it's their first time in London – describe your plan of action.

▸ You have a list of 15 individuals, giving their sex, age and occupation – you can save five of them from nuclear attack – which five and why?

▸ As captain of a football team, inform a member of your team that they have not been selected to play in the final.

▸ Inform your neighbour that you have just (accidentally) run over and killed their cat.

Key competencies

Although some of the above examples may not strike you as directly relevant to medicine, they are assessing one or more of the following eight competencies, which we have developed from the General Medical Council's publication, *Tomorrow's Doctors*:

Academic ability and intellect, empathy, initiative and resilience, communication skills, organisation and problem solving, team work, insight and integrity, effective learning style.

Why MMIs?

Research has shown MMIs to be a better predictor of academic performance and professional behaviour. We piloted MMIs in the 2008/9 academic year and interviewers felt that MMIs were just as fair and accurate as traditional interviews. Interviewees felt that MMIs were fairer and more accurate than traditional interviews.

MMIs allow us to assess more candidates in a shorter period of time, which means you will find out the outcome of your interview sooner.

Subject – personal statement criteria

Directed to UCAS personal statement information

Subject – how it is taught

Integrated to start with and then moves on to problem-/case-based learning from year three.

Test

UKCAT

Any applicants who meet all other minimum requirements and achieves at least 500 in each of the four sections of the UKCAT will be considered for interview. This will be based on the total UKCAT score, which is set after the application closing date.

University College London

Grades

GCSE

All candidates must offer GCSE (or O level from a UK examination board) at grade B or above in both English Language and Mathematics.

UCL expects all UK applicants to offer a modern foreign language at GCSE grade C or equivalent. This requirement does not apply to international students who are already bilingual due to speaking both English and the language of their home country. Candidates may be admitted if they do not offer a modern foreign language GCSE, but would be obliged to take an additional language course during their first year or the preceding summer.

GCSEs will be used as a general indicator of the candidate's academic background.

AS/A level

We require a minimum of three A levels and one additional fourth subject to at least AS level. All AS and A2 components for these four subjects should be completed within two years (Years 12 and 13 at a UK school), with the A2 examinations for the three main A levels all being taken in Year 13.

Chemistry and Biology must be studied at A level. Candidates have a free choice of other subjects, with the following exceptions:

General Studies A level and Critical Thinking A level are acceptable only as alternatives to the additional fourth subject.

Any AS/A level subjects taken in an unusual timeframe (e.g. over more than two years) should be listed on the application, and will of course be considered as part of the overall educational background, but will not count towards the three main A levels that would form an AAA offer. Some candidates may therefore need to take more than three A levels.

Some preference will be given to applicants who offer a contrasting subject at AS/A level. In this context a contrasting subject is one outside the traditional science subjects of Maths, Chemistry, Biology and Physics. For example: English Literature, History, Geography, Art, Music, Religious Studies, Design and Technology or a foreign language etc.

Our standard conditional offer for 2013 entry: grades AAA at A level to include Chemistry and Biology, plus a pass grade in an additional fourth subject to at least AS level.

The UCAS application must list final A level grade predictions (from the referee) along with the actual grades achieved at AS level in Year 12 in order for the candidate to be considered further. Candidates who do not supply AS grades on the UCAS application may be requested to submit these via email. We may also ask some candidates to supply module-level grades or UMS marks. If candidates do not possess AS marks because they are taking their A levels in a linear, rather than modular, format, it is helpful if this is clearly stated in the reference.

Additional A level guidelines

A strong background in both Chemistry and Biology is necessary to ensure that students can cope with the science in our programme; this is why we require both subjects as full A levels. Our expectation is that prospective medical students will excel in these subjects at AS level.

Students who need to re-sit exams in Years 12 and 13 in order to achieve the required grades may struggle subsequently on our programme. Re-sits of January exams the following June are permitted, but we would suggest that candidates who need to re-sit examinations in order to achieve the required grades may not be well-prepared for our programme.

Work experience criteria

Previous experience (both personal and through work experience or volunteering), particularly if it has involved contact with the health care profession or laboratory work, or if the candidate has been involved with the sick, disabled, very young or elderly, and, importantly, is able to reflect on their experiences.

Interview

Interviews last approximately fifteen to twenty minutes and are conducted by a panel of two or three interviewers, including clinical and basic medical science staff, a senior medical student or 'lay' interviewer (e.g., Head of Sixth Form, guest GP). Interviewees will be given a copy of their BMAT essay prior to the interview, as discussion of their essay will form part of the assessment at interview.

Interviewers score the candidate for the following qualities:

▶ intellectual ability (intellectual curiosity and robustness)
▶ motivation for (and understanding of) a career in medicine
▶ awareness of scientific and medical issues
▶ ability to express and defend opinions, including discussion of BMAT essay topic
▶ attitude, including flexibility and integrity
▶ individual strengths (e.g. social, musical, sporting interests or activities)
▶ communication skills (verbal and listening).

Following the interview the recommendations of the interviewers will be reviewed by the admissions tutor and the outcome will be sent to each candidate within two weeks.

It is the policy of this medical school not to reconsider an applicant who has previously been unsuccessful following interview unless they were given specific permission to re-apply.

Subject – personal statement/reference criteria

▶ Previous experience (both personal and through work experience or volunteering), particularly if it has involved contact with the health care profession or laboratory work, or if the candidate has been involved with the sick, disabled, very young or elderly, and, importantly, is able to reflect on their experiences.
▶ Demonstration of motivation to study Medicine and an appropriate attitude.
▶ Other interests, for example music, travel, sports, or any activities that are considered to broaden the general education of the candidate.
▶ Evidence of teamwork, leadership and communication skills.
▶ The referee's assessment of academic ability, study skills, motivation for medicine and personal qualities are taken into account when deciding which candidates to interview.

Subject – how it is taught

Integrated

Test

BMAT

The average test scores for UCL applicants for this 2013 application cycle are 4.5, 4.5 and 3.0 A.

Scores that are above average in each section will strengthen an application but are not a guarantee of success. Scores that are below average in any section will be disadvantageous to an application.

Candidates are asked to note that BMAT scores are not the only factor considered in our selection procedure.

Sample interview questions

▸ When did you first decide you wanted to become a doctor?

▸ What types of career do you think medicine offers?

▸ What are the disadvantages of medicine as a career?

▸ After qualifying as a doctor, how do you go on to become a consultant?

▸ Do you know what an elective is?

▸ What is a physician?

▸ Why medicine? Why not nursing?

▸ Why not another health care profession?

▸ How important is research? Why?

▸ Who sets the curriculum for post-medical training?

▸ What qualities do you have that would contribute to this medical school?

▸ What steps have you taken to ensure that you will be suited to a medical career?

▸ How would you deal with the hard work and commitment needed on a medical course? Are you prepared for six years of study?

▸ Do you think medicine is stressful? How do you deal with stress and pressures?

▸ What do you think your life will be like as a doctor? What are your worries about being a doctor?

▸ How is general practice different from hospital medicine?

▸ What sort of person are you (for example, extrovert or introvert)? What are your good and bad points?

▸ What makes you angry or upset?

▸ What do you do to relax?

▸ Tell us about a problem and how you solved it.

▸ What makes you happy? What makes you sad?

▸ Do you consider yourself to be a perfectionist?

▸ Which do you prefer: conceptual stuff or nitty-gritty things?

▸ Are you more of a scientist or someone who likes working with people?

▸ What would you do if someone you were working with was not pulling their weight in your team?

- What would you do if your patient disagreed with your advice?
- Is there any type of person that you think you would not be able to handle?
- How would you feel treating a child with a terminal illness?
- How would you deal with death?
- If you accidently killed a patient, how would you get over it?
- Can you lead a group, or be part of a group led by someone else?
- What experience do you have of working in teams? Do you prefer working in a team or individually?
- When have you shown leadership/teamwork?
- Do you think medicine is a glamorous career?
- What problems do doctors face today?
- What do patients complain most about regarding doctors?
- Is psychiatry something you would go into?
- How have people's attitudes towards doctors changed in the last fifteen years?
- Do you have a pessimistic or optimistic view of health care in this country?
- What do you think makes a good friend?

- Tell us about your work experience. What did you learn from it?
- Where did you see examples of teamwork?
- How did your work experience prepare you for medicine?
- Tell us about your work shadowing. Have you watched how doctors work?
- Tell us about your voluntary work.
- Have you done any previous research?
- Describe a particular patient you saw on work experience.

- What medical issues have you read about in the news lately?
- Have you read an article about health or medicine lately that has interested you? Tell us about it.
- Were there any ethical issues in the news recently?
- What have you found interesting about medicine or medical ethics recently?
- What medical breakthroughs have taken place in the last 100 years?
- Name and discuss advances in medicine that have happened in the last five years.
- What medical advances do you think will happen in the next ten years?
- How do you think chemistry, biology or maths has influenced medicine in the last twenty years?
- What is the future of transplants?
- What is a retrovirus? How do retroviruses work?
- Do you know how genetic engineering works?
- What ethical problems can you see arising from genetic selection against disease?
- What would you see as the pros and cons of the Internet both for doctors and patients?
- How would you make hospitals more friendly?
- Why are heart diseases in the media more than diarrhoeal diseases when they affect a fifth of the world's population?

▸ Where does money from the NHS come from? Where does it go? How much is spent on the NHS? What is it spent on?

▸ What do you think about the present state of the NHS? What do you think will happen to it in the near future? What do you think about privatising the NHS?

▸ If you had £100 billion to spend on third world health, what would you spend it on?

▸ If you could solve one problem in the NHS, with unlimited resources, what would it be?

▸ If you were head of the NHS what would you spend the money on?

▸ How do you think a surgeon decides who deserves any operation?

▸ How should the NHS cope with an ever-increasing ageing population? What are the issues if everyone lived to 120?

▸ Is it ethical to treat a patient who smokes/drinks/takes drugs?

▸ Imagine you are a GP with a patient who smokes and has been with you for 25 years. He is diagnosed with cancer. What will be running through his mind? He then lowers his head and cries his eyes out. What would you do?

▸ What are the issues with physical contact?

▸ You can only afford one heart operation, but there are two patients – one is fat and smokes, the other is healthy. Who gets the op and why?

▸ Is it right to treat one person and not another? Justify your answer.

▸ How can you justify spending £600,000 treating an overweight, drinking, smoking, middle-aged man instead of improving the health of seventy children?

▸ Do you feel more money needs to be spent on community medicine, i.e., prevention rather than cure?

▸ If a doctor has AIDS should he/she practise medicine?

▸ Does alternative medicine have a place in hospitals?

▸ Do you think people can 'think themselves better'? If so, what is the mechanism for this?

▸ Define empathy. How is it different from sympathy? When would a doctor need to show it? When have you shown empathy? – many follow-up questions

▸ What would you do if a friend's parent divorced? – many follow-up questions

▸ What would you do if the Jehovah's Witness family of a patient refused a blood transfusion?

▸ On what criteria would you base decisions about who to treat and who to turn away?

▸ Who has the final say in a patient's treatment – the doctor, the patient or relatives?

▸ Should we cure people with cancer? Aren't they going to die anyway?

▸ If a child came to you with an injury, with the parents saying she fell, how would you check there was no problem of abuse at home?

▸ Do you agree with testing cosmetics on animals?

▸ Is medicine an art?

▸ Should class A drugs be legalised? (Had five minutes to prepare an answer).

- What is your favourite topic in biology?
- What is the function of the skull? Why do new-born babies not have their skull cages fully fused?
- How do people turn their heads in all directions?
- How does blood get from your toes to your heart? What about at the venae cavae?
- Describe the structure of the heart.
- How does oxygen get from the air to your toes?
- Tell us about haemoglobin and the transportation of oxygen. What effect does high altitude have?
- Describe how air is inhaled and exhaled by mammals.
- What makes the body reject donated organs?
- Describe a neurone. How does an impulse travel down one?
- Why is an old person's long-term memory better than their short-term memory?
- Into what groups can amino acids be divided?
- How would a ketone react with an amine?
- You realise that a patient has been given a double dose of a drug by a doctor. What do you do?
- Why problem-based learning?

Students' comments

▸ *'Be prepared for the usual questions: Why medicine? Why this medical school?'*

▸ *'They seemed concerned about whether you were a normal person, able to cope with work as well as having hobbies, interests, etc.'*

▸ *'They were keen on probing about topical issues. In fact, much of the interview was spent trying to find out what I knew about the political side of medicine.'*

▸ *'I was given a BMJ article to read on cosmetic surgery and asked questions on it.'*

▸ These comments reflect various types of MMI practice:

  • *'Group session first (9 applicants) to discuss a case study: 38 year old morbidly obese woman; what are the possible treatments? Surgery (gastric band), diet and exercise, or group therapy? Each applicant had this info, but also an individual piece of info that others didn't have. 10 minutes thinking time, followed by 20 minutes to discuss. Each applicant told to include their own info and then reach group conclusion – 3 observers.'*

  • *'Group discussion – 9 people. Given 10 minutes to read through and write notes on a problem with 3 options to solve it E.g. man has cancer – possible treatments: withhold treatment, hormone therapy or surgery. Each candidate had a different piece of additional information – 20 minutes to discuss and reach conclusion.'*

▸ *'3 x 8 minute interviews: first based on group session; second – ethics question above; third – based on personal statement.'*

▸ *'3 mini-tests – 1 on group discussion, 1 on work experience, 1 with dealing with stress and struggles with PBL (Problem Based Learning). What would you find the hardest?'*

▸ *'Group discussion: 3 mini interviews (7 minutes each) – 1 on group discussion, 1 on personal statement, 1 on ethical dilemma in recent news. Pros, cons and own opinion. Felt interviewer was very harsh and cold – seemed as if it was a waste of their (interviewer's) time. No support/help if stuck with a question.'*

▸ *'4 x 6 minute interviews with 2 minutes to read a brief before each interview. One of the tasks involved analysing the results of a clinical trial and involved calculations and questions about the significance of data.'*

6 ▶ A realistic application to Oxbridge

Never, in the history of education, has so much hot air been expended on a single issue. Rather than adding to the global warming attributable to this subject, this is our attempt to deconstruct what is really going on. It is written presuming the reader is a teacher or careers advisor who has recently been given responsibility for students who might be considering an Oxbridge application.

A framework to help your students

A helpful acronym

In careers guidance, if we are trying to make something more understandable, our first tactic is to create an acronym. This will hopefully remind you of the issues you need to be aware of to help your possible Oxbridge applicants:

G	–	Grades
R	–	Reading
I	–	Interview
S	–	Subject
T	–	Tests

The phrase 'grist to the mill' refers to turning something to one's profit or advantage. Turning the resources available in the sixth form to the student's advantage is exactly what is required for a successful Oxbridge application and is what will be addressed in this section.

Grades

We need to ensure that possible candidates have a realistic idea of what GCSE, AS and A level (or equivalent qualification) grades or scores are typical of a successful Oxbridge applicant and that they receive this information in time to act on it. Some would argue that by being specific about grades we could be putting off talented potential applicants. We would disagree. In practice we need clarity, not ambiguity.

▶ **Typical GCSE grades**

Both Cambridge and Oxford are now openly saying that the average applicant has five to eight A*s at GCSE. Moreover, Cambridge is saying that even if the applicant has been to a challenging school they normally have three to four A*s – and quite often more. There can be exceptions, but the person doing the reference must be prepared to give comparative evidence as to why the student is an exception and refer to compensatory and contextual factors.

▶ **Typical AS grades**

Getting A grades at AS level is not normally enough. For Cambridge they need to be high A grades. Applicants with UMS averages below 90% in their three best or most relevant subjects might not be called for interview, especially for the most competitive subjects. Oxford seems to be placing more emphasis on the performance in tests (see below), although in reality their applicants will have similar UMS scores. Please remember that Cambridge applicants have to declare their AS level UMS scores on the online supplementary form but Oxford applicants do not. Normally, most candidates declare individual AS module grades unless it is explicitly stated, by the referee, that it is school policy not to take AS exams in Year 12.

▸ **Typical A Level grades**

Cambridge asks in the main for a standard A*AA. All Oxford courses, in the area of Medicine, Physical and Life sciences will be asking for A* grades for students applying for 2014 entry, with A*A*A required for most Mathematics courses. Always check details in the online Cambridge and Oxford prospectuses. If you want a real eye-opener, check UCAS Tariff scores for Oxford and Cambridge degrees in **www.unistats.com**. The average applicant, to whom an offer was made from Oxford in 2012, went on to achieve 2.3 A* grades.

When writing a reference for an applicant you should place his or her academic ability in the context of where they stand in comparison to the rest of the year group. Any other contextual information could also be usefully added.

Reading

Possible applicants need to understand that they will have to read more widely than for most other university interviews, be prepared to analyse what they have read and offer a critique. Some students may need help with choosing texts or, in maths and the sciences, practising problems. The more they read and do that is related to their subject the more they will have to say in their personal statement.

It is essential:

▸ that the student learns that, without wider reading or subject-related activity, they will have very little evidence to back up their claim to be interested and engaged in their subject

▸ that the student understands how the admissions tutor is likely to look for salient points in the personal statement as possible embarkation points for deeper questioning in the interview

▸ that he or she learns that anything that is put in the statement can lead to a question that may be followed up with others on the same topic

▸ that the student learns to talk and discuss issues with friends, teachers and family.

The importance of critical and analytical reading beyond the confines of an A level syllabus cannot be stressed enough.

Interview

It is crucial that possible applicants are given tasks:

▸ that give them experience of dealing with subject-based questions and how they need to engage in the interview (by engage, we mean answering questions that arise from the answers they gave to the original question from the interviewer)

▸ that make them think for themselves rather than regurgitate what they have been taught by a teacher

▸ that make them realise that they need to understand fully what each of them has written in his or her personal statement, a copy of which must be kept to refer to ahead of interviews. In addition they must understand that not being able to talk in detail about what they have written is likely to be interpreted as a lack of motivation or commitment.

> ▸ that help them to learn how admissions tutors will focus upon salient points in the statement as possible topics to bring up.
>
> ▸ that try to replicate the interview experience. Applicants should have a mock interview, preferably with someone who is knowledgeable on the subject and whom they do not know well. They should also watch videos produced by, for example, Oriel College Oxford and Emmanuel College Cambridge to gain a clearer understanding of the interview process.

We feel very strongly that applicants, especially from non-selective state schools, will often have no experience of being interrogated on an academic issue. They may answer questions in class but they will not normally have had to face further questioning on their original answer. All applicants must be exposed to appropriate questioning related to their subject in a mock interview scenario. A useful way of looking at an Oxbridge interview is as 'an exam paper out loud.' Once applicants have an awareness of what the interview experience will be like, they should put their efforts into wider reading around their subject. This is much more important than doing repeated mock interviews. Extra-curricular activities that do not relate to the subject applied for will not be used in the selection process. No need to be a rounded student good at sport and music, this isn't what the tutors are looking for as it doesn't tell them much about their potential for studying, for example, biochemistry.

Subject

Candidates need to understand why they are applying for their chosen subject. Mainly the subject should relate to their abilities and interests, but it could also relate to their values (Politics for example). Obsessive enthusiasm backed by evidence of serious interest is the only way forward here. One Oxford tutor has told us with 'due humour' that in this context 'geekiness IS good!'

Students need to understand that they will mainly be asked subject-based questions, with the possible starting points being:

▸ something extracted from the personal statement

▸ a piece of marked work (possibly in a different subject than that for which they are applying to study)

▸ something that has been covered in the A level syllabus but which is then extended and developed. This type of questioning is intended to test how students can think for themselves and how they can apply their existing knowledge to new situations.

Tests

Potential applicants need to know that they may have to take additional tests either at school or at the interview and they need to have experience of being exposed to what is involved.

They may face a formal test (the Oxford or Cambridge thinking skills assessment (TSA – for Cambridge this can cover subjects such as Computing, Engineering and sometimes PPS and Land Economy; for Oxford this covers PPE, Economics and Management, Experimental Psychology, Psychology and Philosophy and, in the future, Geography), English Literature admissions test (ELAT at Oxford), Biomedical admissions test (BMAT at both), Sixth Term Examination Paper (STEP at Cambridge for Maths), LNAT: the national admissions test for law at Oxford and the Cambridge Law Admission Test, history aptitude test at Oxford (HAT), Maths, Physics, Computing and probably in the future Engineering, face a formal Maths or Physics test at Oxford) or an informal test (an unseen poem, some text in a foreign language, a scientific problem, a piece of historical text at both Oxford and Cambridge depending on the subject applied for). Overall, Oxford seems to have more formal tests whereas Cambridge has more informal tests and also wants more in-depth information on AS level performance.

Students need to familiarise themselves with the content and style of any formal tests and be informed of the relevant website details. We feel it is important that students are given the formal tests in a mock exam situation and, where possible, that their answers are marked so they have a realistic idea of how they did. All the websites for the above tests have examples of past/sample papers.

All the information on tests is collated at:
www.ox.ac.uk/admissions/undergraduate_courses/how_to_apply/tests/index.html
www.cam.ac.uk/admissions/undergraduate/courses

The really important preparation is for the candidate to be aware of the style and format of the questions, which don't look like A level in many cases, and the time allowed for each element of the tests.

The student should practise dealing with related unfamiliar texts, articles or problems even if they do not face a formal test. There may well be an informal test at interview.

Contextual issues and student background

All of the above presumes that the applicant has, of their own free will, decided that they want to apply for an Oxford or Cambridge college. It does not try to deal with the wider issues of encouraging students to apply to Oxbridge. Nor does it address the perceived social injustices of the education system that Oxford and Cambridge universities are often accused of maintaining. Please do not confuse the applicant with the sociology of education issues that often come up in the media relating to Oxbridge application. These issues will be irrelevant to the applicant and will divert them from the GRIST framework.

Other issues such as college choice, understanding the Cambridge supervision system, the Oxford tutorial system and finding out contextual information that can be passed on to the Cambridge and Oxford colleges, should be covered with possible applicants. But we would argue that they are not as important as the above issues in the GRIST framework. See 'Other points to consider' below.

Many organisations offer to help improve an applicant's chance of getting into Oxbridge. They often charge fees and you should be aware of the danger of over-preparation. We would argue that all they are doing is implementing elements of the GRIST framework, which can be done at a school or local authority level with the support of Oxford and Cambridge Universities themselves. We would also argue that Oxford and Cambridge Universities methods of selections are as fair, or in fact fairer, than other common selection processes used by other universities, as they use a wider range of methods to make their final selection. *However*, one obvious weakness in the Oxbridge and Cambridge universities' methods of selection is that there is not 'equality of preparation'. This clearly varies between schools and areas. It is therefore for schools, local authorities and Oxbridge themselves, to help implement the GRIST framework and work towards 'equality of preparation'. To be fair, Oxford and Cambridge Universities do recognise this criticism and adjust their approaches accordingly.

Oxford currently collects six pieces of information for all UK domiciled candidates attending UK schools and colleges, all of which we are able to get through the UCAS application:

Educational Factors:

Pre-16 qualifications – school performing below the national (i.e. English, Welsh, NI or Scottish) average.

Post-16 qualifications – school or college performing below the national average.

School or College with limited success in securing offers from Oxford.

Postcode Factors:

Candidate lives in a postcode with evidence of high socio-economic disadvantage using ACORN dataset.

Candidate lives in a postcode with evidence of low progression to Higher Education (POLAR).

In-care:

Candidate has indicated they have been in care for a period of at least three months (subsequently will be verified with the referee).

Where a candidate has been in care, or has at least one postcode and one educational factor, this gives tutors a strong recommendation to interview, provided that the candidate is predicted to achieve the necessary grades to meet the standard offer, and has not performed too poorly in any required admissions aptitude test.

Other points to consider

What makes Oxford and Cambridge Universities different?

> - The quality of the educational experience. Students will often be taught by the 'leaders in their fields' and, in return, they will have to push themselves to achieve very high levels of work. It should not be forgotten that there is, of course, academic excellence at other universities as well.
> - More teaching is done individually. Students are expected to be self-starters and work independently.
> - Whatever the degree, Oxbridge graduates have very good career prospects. A certain level of respect from employers is gained simply because of the university attended (although this effect diminishes over time).
> - Colleges are normally friendly places, in pleasant surroundings. Accommodation provision is often very good. A close college community provides a friendly and welcoming home for students who are living away for the first time. Students soon get to know one another other, and tutors get to know students individually, enabling them to respond to their individual academic needs. Oxbridge colleges still have a better level of funding than other universities, including generous bursary schemes such as the Oxford Opportunity Bursary and the Moritz-Heyman Scholarships.

What potential candidates need to know about the college system

- Oxford University and Cambridge University each have well over 20 colleges. Students should not be put off by some idiosyncratic pronunciations. Magdalene College, for example, is pronounced maud-lin.

- Lectures are taught by the university. English lectures, for example, will be taught at the university's English faculty. Tutorials (at Oxford) and supervisions (at Cambridge) involve being taught individually or in small groups at the student's own college. As the student specialises in later years of their course the tutorials will often be with tutors at other Colleges – this is important because it means that a student shouldn't feel that they have to be a student at the College that has the 'world expert' in their subject – if they take a course that they supervise then they are likely to have them as a tutor.

- Undergraduates live, eat and socialise at their colleges, in the main. Cambridge colleges, on the whole, will find accommodation for three years. Oxford colleges vary. Very few students are in private rented accommodation as undergraduates – they are usually 'living out' in College-owned houses in second year.

- It is unusual for two people from the same school to apply for the same subject at the same college.

Points for students to consider when choosing a college at Oxbridge

- Does the college offer accommodation for the duration of the course?

- Does the college have a fellow or director of studies in the relevant subject? Students should research the college that interests them most, but not become too attached. Applications may be pooled and an offer come from another college. About 25% of students receive an offer from a college that was not their first preference at Oxford.

- *Students cannot apply to both Oxford and Cambridge.*

▶ Accountancy

(Also Banking, Finance and Insurance)

Essential A levels: None.

Useful A levels (possibly): Maths and Economics.

Chance of being interviewed: Most applicants are offered places on the basis of what is in UCAS Apply, but there is a chance you may be interviewed. Some top firms are now offering school leaver programmes, which incorporate a BSc. For these you will almost certainly have an interview that may replicate their graduate recruitment process. www.directions.org.uk

What you need to know

▶ An accountancy course will not train you to become a professional in the field: You will still have to complete professional qualifications after your degree. However, you will normally be exempted from some parts of the professional course.

▶ You should try to get some work experience in a finance-related industry. Identify what you have learned from the experience in order to discuss it in an interview.

▶ Make sure you have some understanding of what the industries of accountancy, finance, insurance and banking involve and be clear about why you want to work in them. For example, accountancy is concerned with the management of money, but a degree may not just lead to a job as a chartered accountant; graduates may go into high finance, or general management, or become entrepreneurs.

▶ Find out as much as you can from the websites of the industries' professional bodies listed here.

Accountancy
The Institute of Chartered Accountants in England and Wales: www.icaew.com
The Association of Chartered Certified Accountants: www.accaglobal.com
The Chartered Institute of Management Accountants: www.cimaglobal.com
The Chartered Institute of Public Finance and Accountancy: www.cipfa.org

Retail banking
IFS School of Finance: ifslearning.ac.uk
Building Societies Association: www.bsa.org.uk

Investment and Corporate Banking
British Bankers' Association: www.bba.org.uk

Insurance
The Chartered Insurance Institute: www.cii.co.uk

For all areas
www.directions.org.uk

Sample interview questions

▸ What is the difference between a certified and a management accountant?
▸ What is accountancy?

▸ Why does a career in accountancy/banking/insurance interest you?
▸ Why do you want to do this degree rather than a business studies degree?
▸ If you can become an accountant after any degree, why do you want to specialise now?

▸ What is auditing?
▸ What is management consultancy?
▸ Who is to blame for the credit crunch?

▸ Have you looked at any of the websites of the professional bodies? What did you find out?
▸ What did the accountancy firm you visited on your work experience do? Who were its clients?
▸ What is your back up to this course?
▸ Do you know what you have to do after your degree to qualify?

▸ Actuarial Science/Studies

Essential A levels: Maths.

Useful A levels (possibly): Further Maths and Economics.

Chance of being interviewed: Many applicants will be offered places on the basis of what is in UCAS Apply, but some applicants are interviewed.

What you need to know

▸ Actuaries calculate insurance and pension risks using statistical techniques.
▸ You need to be very good at maths and very interested in financial issues.
▸ You will need to stick at it: You will have more years of professional training after graduation.
▸ Try to meet an actuary and talk to them about what the job involves.
▸ Visit **www.actuaries.org.uk**

Sample interview questions

▸ What are the tasks of an actuary?
▸ Why do you want be an actuary?

▸ What are your favourite areas of maths and why?
▸ What did you learn from your work experience with the pensions company?
▸ What are the organisations that are responsible for regulating the UK financial system?
▸ How does an ageing population affect the pensions industry?
▸ What are the insurance implications of higher levels of car crime in some inner-city areas?
▸ From what you have studied in A level maths, can you think of a possible statistical method to help us calculate car insurance premiums?

▶ Agriculture

What you need to know

▸ You should have work experience in farming.

▸ You must be up to date with current political and economic issues in farming.

▸ Visit: **www.ukagriculture.com**

▸ Lantra is the Sector Skills Council for the environmental and land-based sector, representing seventeen industries across the whole of the United Kingdom, including: land management and production; animal health and welfare; and environmental industries. Visit **www.lantra.co.uk**

▸ Look at the sample interview questions under: 'Biology', 'Business studies' and 'Veterinary science'.

▶ American Studies

Essential A levels: Requirements vary, but English and History are often asked for.

Useful A levels (possibly): Politics.

Chance of being interviewed: Interviews are more common than for other humanities degrees. This is because people often have misconceptions about the course they are applying for.

What you need to know

▸ If you want to study some literature, some history and some politics, and get to study at a foreign university, then this could be the course for you.

▸ Courses vary. Some offer the chance to study film, music or visual arts. Others are more like a traditional English or History degree. Make sure you know which you are applying for.

▸ Expect questions on American Literature that you have read (questions will mostly be based on what you have put in your personal statement).

▸ Expect questions on American history.

▸ If there is an American election pending, or if there has just been one, it is a good idea to demonstrate analytical reading of relevant press coverage.

▸ Visit: **www.americansc.org.uk**

Sample interview questions

▸ Do you have any personal or family reasons for wanting to do American studies?

▸ Do you think American culture is overwhelming British culture?

▸ What do you think are the social problems facing the USA today?

▸ What American literature have you read away from your set texts?

▸ Will J D Salinger be remembered in 200 years time? Why or why not? What about Jack Kerouac?

▸ What was the context in which John Steinbeck wrote *The Grapes of Wrath*?

▸ What current American political issues interest you?

▸ What are the differences between the Democrats and the Republicans?

▸ What do you hope to gain from your time at an American university?

▸ Do you know which American and Canadian universities are linked with our university?

▸ Do you think the UK will ever have a black prime minister?

▸ What are the similarities and differences between the US involvement in Vietnam and Afghanistan?

▸ The US Constitution enshrines the concept of individual liberty. Is this, in your view, more important than the impact of gun crime?

▸ Anatomy

See sample interview questions under: **'Biology'**, **'Medicine'** *and* **'Physiology'**.

▸ Animal Sciences

What you need to know

▸ Look at the sample interview questions under: 'Biology' and 'Veterinary science'.

▸ For specialist courses, such as equine science and animal welfare management, relevant work experience or voluntary work will be vital.

▸ Lantra is the Sector Skills Council for the environmental and land-based sector, representing seventeen industries across the whole of the United Kingdom, including: land management and production; animal health and welfare; environmental and industries. Visit: www.lantra.co.uk

▸ Anthropology

Essential A levels: None.

Useful A levels (possibly): For a small number of courses, Sociology or a science A level such as Biology is helpful.

Chance of being interviewed: Many applicants will be offered places on the basis of what is in UCAS Apply, but some courses do still interview.

What you need to know

▸ Be very clear in your own mind that you understand what anthropology is. It is the study of human behaviour, beliefs, institutions and the various societies in which people live.

▸ Think about whether you are interested in the social or biological aspects of anthropology, or both.

▸ Interviews will tend to focus on comments made in your personal statement.

▸ Interviewers are looking for evidence of interest (books you have read, museums you have visited and overseas visits). If you have travelled abroad, can you compare other societies with your own?

‣ Check if the course will involve field work and whether you will be funded to do this.

‣ Be prepared to examine an object.

‣ Visit: **www.discoveranthropology.org.uk**

Sample interview questions

‣ What made you decide to apply for anthropology?

‣ Have any of your A level subjects influenced your interest and why?

‣ What do you read when you are not studying?

‣ What tensions do you think the Inuit deal with?

‣ Do all societies have heroes?

‣ Why do we need laws?

‣ How has life changed for men in the last fifty years?

‣ Why do some societies try to impose their values and beliefs on to others?

‣ Tell me about water irrigation in North Africa.

‣ What are the primary societies studied by anthropologists?

‣ What impact has globalisation had on anthropological studies?

‣ If an alien came to earth how would you explain the differences between people and animals?

‣ Can you truly gain an insight into a civilisation through the lives of normal people?

‣ Do normal people in different societies really live such different lives from one another?

‣ Is the evolution of visual culture linked to Darwin's theory of evolution?

‣ Does visual culture have anything to do with survival of the fittest?

‣ How does secularism affect different parts of the world?

‣ Have humans stopped evolving?

Students' comments

‣ *'I was surprised that I wasn't asked at all why I wanted to study anthropology. I also didn't talk about much of what was in my statement or my essay, and they seemed not to want me to refer to ideas in the books I had read, even specifically asking me not to at one point.'*

‣ *'I felt they were deliberately testing me on things I didn't know, so it is difficult to tell if I gave them good enough answers.'*

‣ *'I was given an object and asked to interpret what it might indicate about a society.'*

‣ Archaeology

Essential A levels: None.

Chance of being interviewed: While many courses will make you an offer on the basis of what is in UCAS Apply, a significant minority will interview.

What you need to know

‣ Really do try and get some experience of excavations and digs (visit: **www.archeologyuk.org**).

‣ Do as much introductory reading about archaeology as you can.

▸ Think about how the study of archaeology helps us to understand history.

▸ If the course involves overseas trips, will financial help be available?

Sample interview questions

▸ Why do you want to do a course in archaeology?

▸ Which do you prefer: archaeology or prehistory?

▸ Do people learn from history?

▸ Why should money be spent on archaeology when medicine needs so much?

▸ Why should taxpayers spend several thousand pounds a year for you to study archaeology?

▸ Who cares if evidence of an ancient basket-weaving tribe is found in southern Italy?

▸ How can we date artefacts? Are there any other methods besides radiocarbon dating?

▸ What are the arguments for and against keeping the Parthenon Marbles (Elgin Marbles) at the British Museum?

▸ What countries have you travelled to? What did you learn from your experiences?

▸ Have you visited any archaeological sites? Which ones?

▸ If you were given £1 million to excavate an archaeological site would you focus on the relics of the elite or the commoners?

Student's comment

▸ *'There were (luckily) few questions about archaeology itself and nothing on ancient history. The interviewer did, however, give me an address to contact when I said I wanted to go on a dig in my year off.'*

▸ Architecture

Essential A levels: For a small number of degree courses Art is required. Some universities ask for an arts/science mix. NB: *A portfolio of drawings and ideas is often essential.*

Useful A levels (possibly): Art, Maths and Physics.

Chance of being interviewed: Many courses will interview and inspect portfolios but the number that are doing this is declining.

What you need to know

▸ It is essential to show an interest in the history of architecture (for example, classical Greek and Roman, Gothic, organic and international styles) and the work and influence of architects such as Vitruvius, William of Sens, Frank Lloyd Wright and Le Corbusier. There are many books on this but a good starting point is *The Story of Architecture* by Jonathan Glancey.

▸ You must have a portfolio of drawings including your own ideas for buildings and drawings of existing buildings. Other artwork could be included as an addition.

▸ You must be able to talk about your ideas. Think about the three elements of design: the look, the cost and the making. Be prepared to be shown photographs, drawings, etc., as a starting point.

- You will need to have confirmed your commitment to a career in architecture through work experience.
- Remember that architecture is a multi-disciplinary profession requiring a combination of artistic, technological and sociological expertise. The challenge of architecture is to produce, within a given budget, an aesthetically pleasing design that will stand up to wear and tear and is the kind of building people would like to live and/or work in.
- Visit the website of the Royal Institute of British Architects (RIBA): **www.architecture.com**
- Visit: **www.greatbuildings.com**

The annual Stirling Prize for architecture is awarded in the autumn every year. There is intense coverage in the press. Keep a cuttings file to give you ideas to discuss.

Sample interview questions

- Why do you want to study architecture? How long have you wanted to be an architect?
- Architecture is an underpaid and overworked profession, so why do you want to go into it?
- Schools of architecture each have their own strengths and specialities. Why did you choose to apply to study architecture at this particular university?

- Are there any buildings that have particularly influenced you?
- Do you have a favourite contemporary architect? Who is it and why?
- Describe a building that you like, of any style or period.

- What do you know about the architectural styles of the 18th and 19th centuries, i.e. neoclassicism, the Gothic revival and romantic architecture?
- Describe the front of St Paul's Cathedral in London.

- Have you read any books about architecture? Which ones?
- How have you tried to broaden your knowledge and understanding of architecture?
- Do you think your A levels are relevant to studying architecture?

- Do you think new skyscrapers in London have enhanced the beauty of the city? If so, why? if not, why not?
- How do you think office blocks should be designed?
- Do you have anything against buildings showing their structures outwardly?
- Finland has a much higher percentage of women architects than Britain. Why do you think that is?

- Why are you interested in landscape architecture?
- Do you think community landscaping is important? Why?

Students' comments

- *'I was asked to solve some 3D problems on a piece of paper, which I couldn't do, but the interviewer refused to let me give up until I'd at least got close. As a result I spent about ten to fifteen minutes on two problems.'*
- *'While I showed the interviewer my portfolio he maintained a perfectly blank expression and made no comments.'*
- *'I was asked very specific questions about periods of architectural history, which is hard with a subject like architecture because you don't study it at school. These questions only show how well you've been drilled for the interview, not whether you will be a creative and good architecture student.'*

‣ *'I was told in a letter about the interview to be prepared to answer questions on modern architecture, construction and the building industry, but none was asked. However, the interviewer was very interested in all the artwork in my portfolio.'*

‣ *'Just before my interview I was asked to read an article on the Architecture of Schools, which I was then questioned on.'*

‣ Art and Design

Essential A levels: Art or Design A level/Other relevant qualifications. These will allow you to build up the portfolio you need to get on to an art foundation course. NB: Most entrants to art and design degrees will have done a one-year art foundation course after their A levels. Some art and design students gain entry to higher education courses without doing a foundation course. Some portfolios are now reviewed online through Flickr.

What you need to know

Mostly, artistic sixth-form students take Art A level, which is the study of painting, drawing and sculpture. Yet most university students in this field study design subjects such as graphic design, fashion design, product design and interior design. An art foundation course acts as a bridge between A levels and design degrees.

The normal attributes of an art foundation course are as follows:

‣ It is one year long, full time.

‣ Fees are not normally charged if you take the course while you are still eighteen years old.

‣ In the first term you will try out all the major areas of design – graphic, fashion, product, interior and others depending on the course.

‣ In the second term you will try to decide which area of art and design you would like to specialise in. You will begin to concentrate on this area so that you have a specialist portfolio ready for the degree/foundation degree or HND course you wish to apply for.

‣ You will be expected to work hard on your drawing skills throughout the course.

‣ It is a very intense year and it is not an easy option. By the time you have completed the course you should know whether art and design is for you or not. If you feel that you do not want to do a degree in art or design then you can apply for other degrees on the strength of the A levels that you have.

‣ It is very common for students to start an art foundation course thinking that they want to do a certain sort of design (for example, fashion) and then, once they have tried out everything else, to decide to do something different (for example, illustration).

‣ Most art and design degrees and HND courses make the successful completion of an art foundation course an entry requirement.

Visit the websites of the National Society for Education in Art & Design (**www.nsead.org**), the Design Council (**www.designcouncil.org.uk**) and the Creative and Cultural Skills Council (**www.ccskills.org.uk**).

Sample interview questions

- How did you design and make some of the pieces in your portfolio? Why did you choose a particular style?
- Which is your favourite piece of work from your portfolio?
- What do you think is good about your drawing?
- What motivates and inspires you?
- Which aspects of the art foundation course do you particularly wish to pursue?
- What kind of career are you considering after completing your art foundation course?

- What examples of industrial design inspire you?
- What types of graphic design interest you? Give me examples.
- Choose a piece in your portfolio. Why have you selected it?
- Is fine art design?
- Which fashion designers have you looked at? What is different about their work?
- How many sections will you need to make this garment?
- Tell me about a recent exhibition you went to. How did it influence your work, if at all?
- Who are your favourite artists?

Transport Product Design

- How is your maths?
- Do you think you will be able to cope with the engineering?
- Questions on portfolio – ability to develop ideas.

Students' comments

- *'There were no questions, just a review of my portfolio. It is really important to make sure all your good work is in your portfolio, and to include a wide range of work.'*
- *'It wasn't really like an interview. We had a group talk about the textile design course and then we were shown round the department. Then they saw us individually but there were no questions. They just told us what they thought of our portfolios.'*
- *'I was left feeling in great doubt about the quality of my work.'*
- *'One thing that I was quite pleased about was that the interviewer told me what was good and bad about my work. He told me how I could improve my style in my year off.'*
- *'This university only interviews students who do not meet all of academic requirements, but that they are nevertheless interested in. Keen to see photos of final pieces in portfolio not just working drawings.'*

▸ Astronomy

What you need to know

▸ Look at the sample interview questions under: *'Physics'* and *'Maths'*.

▸ Wider reading and visits to observatories will be important.

▸ Biochemistry

See sample interview questions under: 'Biology', 'Chemistry', 'Natural Sciences' and 'Physiology'.

▸ Biology/Biochemistry/ Biotechnology/Botany

Biology
Essential A levels: Biology and Chemistry.

Useful A levels (possibly): Maths or Physics.

Chance of being interviewed: Most courses will make you an offer on the basis of what is in UCAS Apply but a significant minority of courses still interview.

Biochemistry
Essential A levels: Always Chemistry. Some degrees will say you must have biology as well. Others will ask for chemistry plus one of Maths, Physics or Biology. Doing Chemistry, Biology and Maths or Physics will keep all Biochemistry courses open to you.

What you need to know

▸ Biochemistry is the study of biology at a molecular level.

▸ Look at the sample questions under: **'Biology'**, **'Chemistry'**, **'Natural Sciences'** and **'Physiology'**.

▸ You need to be fascinated by the living world and have examples to prove this that you can talk about in the interview.

▸ Questions will cover topics that you have already studied for your biology A level.

▸ Degree courses can involve much independent research, so examples of your interest in biology outside of school will be useful.

▸ If you are applying for a more specialist course (for example, botany) can you explain why?

▸ Visit the website: **www.societyofbiology.org**

▸ Visit the website of the Biochemical Society: **www.biochemistry.org**

▸ Cogent is the Sector Skills Council for the chemicals and pharmaceuticals, oil and gas, petroleum and polymer industries. Visit: **www.cogent-ssc.com**

Sample interview questions

- Why do you enjoy biology and which aspects of the subject do you like most?
- Why didn't you apply to study medicine, rather than anatomy and developmental biology?
- You want to study cell biology, so why are you not taking chemistry A level?
- What kind of career are you interested in pursuing after your degree?
- Tell us about the field work you have done for your biology and geography A levels.
- How do enzymes work?
- How do mutations affect bonding and folding amino acids?
- Explain how gel electrophoresis works.
- What bonding takes place within individual DNA nucleotide bases?
- Are you more interested in biochemistry than any other biological science? – from personal statement.
- Tell us about one main theory of cell biology.
- Why do you think free-living chloroplasts 'decided' to form into membrane-bound cells?
- How can you show the differences between a free-living chloroplast and one from a cell?
- Describe the structure of an amino acid. What are the properties of the amino and carboxyl groups? Tell us about the formation of peptide bonds.
- What do you know about protein folding?
- Describe the structure of DNA.
- Tell us about the sequencing of the human genome. What else do you know about the human genome project?
- What features make fungi different?

- In the study of human sciences, how can you make a connection between economics and biology?
- Can theories in economics and biology fully mix in a society?
- How is maths used in biology? Is it important?
- Why are you interested in epidemiology?

- What articles have you read in the *New Scientist*?
- What do you think about human cloning and other biology-related issues currently in the news?
- What do you think about animal/human dissection?
- How would you go about curing cancer?
- What nutritional problems are caused by famine?
- What are the issues when a society relies on one main type of foodstuff?
- What are the benefits of genetically modified foods? Are there disadvantages?
- What do you think is the value of gardening programmes?
- Tell us what you know about acid rain.
- What is the difference between nature studies and ecology?
- How do you investigate animal behaviour experimentally?
- Look at this object [an elephant's tooth]. Guess what it is.

Students' comments

- *'The two interviewers began by quizzing me on A level biology concepts by asking me straightforward questions and getting me to draw things on the blackboard. Then they threw in some difficult, advanced chemistry and expected me to take the discussion to a biochemistry degree level. I was not able to do this well at all and I had to say "I don't know" many times.*

Much of the interview was spent with them explaining principles of biochemistry to me, which I still found very difficult to follow.'

▸ *'I was shown round the whole department and asked if I had seen such equipment before. Everything was explained to me, but if I had known beforehand what equipment I would be shown it would have helped.'*

▸ *'We were shown a lot of the labs, but it was very much a case of "look but don't touch". A lot of the equipment was very expensive.'*

▸ *'When he asked me about acid rain I couldn't answer sufficiently and so I asked him to explain to me so that I learned something. He seemed pleased by the fact that I wanted to learn.'*

▸ *'Confirmed I understood what was required on course including work ethic. Interview was quite informal. Given offer at end of interview.'*

▸ Biotechnology

See sample interview questions under: **'Biology'**, **'Chemistry'**, **'Natural Sciences'** *and* **'Physiology'**.

▸ Botany

See sample interview questions under: **'Biology'**, **'Chemistry'**, **'Natural Sciences'** *and* **'Physiology'**.

▸ Building

What you need to know

▸ Also consider courses in Building Services Engineering.

▸ You should have a clear idea about why you want to enter this career field and evidence to support this (for example, work experience or talks with building professionals).

▸ Look at the sample interview questions under: **'Architecture'**, **'Engineering'** and **'Surveying'**.

▸ Visit the websites **www.ciob.org.uk** and **www.bconstructive.co.uk**

Sample interview questions

▸ Tell me about a construction project in your local area.

▸ How do you know that you can lead a team?

▸ What are some of the different jobs that are in the building industry?

▸ Are you prepared to travel with your work?

Business Studies and Management

Essential A levels: None.

Useful A levels (possibly): Maths, Business Studies and Economics.

Chance of being interviewed: Most courses will make offers on the basis of what is in UCAS Apply.

What you need to know

▸ The subjects that are always studied for these degrees are: Economics, Human Resources, Marketing, Accounting, Finance, and, usually, Quantitative Methods (Statistics) and IT. Try to get across to an interviewer that you can cope with a wide range of subjects.

▸ Do not be concerned about the plethora of different course names: Business Studies, Business and Management, Business Management, Management Studies, Business Administration, Commerce and so on. They are all essentially the same thing.

▸ Some courses allow you to specialise in a particular field (for example, marketing) by the end of the course. Others stay general to the end.

▸ Think about your personal qualities and what you have learned from any work experience or part-time work you have done. Any evidence of working in a team would be particularly useful.

▸ Visit the Chartered Management Institute website: **www.managers.org.uk**

▸ Other websites to visit include: the Financial Skills Partnership, **www.financialskillspartnership.org.uk** and **www.directions.org.uk** and that of People 1st, the Sector Skills Council for the hospitality, leisure, retail, travel and tourism industries. People 1st covers: contract food service providers, events, gambling, holiday parks, hospitality services, hostels, hotels, membership clubs, pubs, bars and nightclubs, restaurants, self-catering accommodation, tourist services, travel services, retail services and visitor attractions. Visit: **www.people1st.co.uk** and **www.uksp.co.uk**

▸ SkillsActive is the Sector Skills Council for the active leisure and learning industry embracing sport and fitness, outdoors and adventure, playwork, camping and caravanning. Visit: **www.skillsactive.com**

Sample interview questions

▸ Why do you want to study business when your A levels are not directly linked to it?
▸ What specific areas of business are you interested in and why?

▸ Define marketing.
▸ What types of marketing are there?
▸ Could you market a product or service you do not believe in?
▸ What is direct marketing?
▸ Do you know what below-the-line marketing is?
▸ What do you think will be the most important industries in Britain in the next decade and after?
▸ What do you think about Sunday trading?
▸ What is the difference between a clearing bank and an investment bank?
▸ How can businesses make money out of leisure time?
▸ Is the customer always right?

▸ What qualities should a manager have?

▸ What skills are needed in hospitality management?

▸ What role does teamwork play in hospitality management?

▸ Can you think of examples of good and bad restaurant management?

▸ Tell us about any work experience you have had.

▸ Have you done any part-time work? If so, how would you improve the company you worked for?

▸ Do you think large supermarkets are a good or bad thing for customers? How do they affect town centres?

▸ Why are some people unhappy in their jobs even when they are paid well?

▸ You say you want to be an entrepreneur! What's your big idea then?

Students' comments

▸ *'Apart from the actual interview there was also a group discussion session, where they monitored our behaviour and reactions within a group.'*

▸ *'We were placed in groups of five and each group was assigned a first-year student to be with us for the day. In the afternoon my group had to go into a room and discuss a particular issue, while the student, a lecturer and a retailer quietly listened and observed us.'*

▸ Chemistry/Chemical Engineering

See sample interview questions under: **'Natural Sciences'** *and* **'Physics'**.

Essential A levels: Chemistry and usually Maths or Physics. Some courses ask for Chemistry, Maths and Physics, while some prefer Chemistry, Maths and Biology.

Chance of being interviewed: Most universities will make offers based on the content of the UCAS Apply, but a significant minority still interview, especially for four-year MSc courses, many of which have a year in industry.

What you need to know

▸ You will probably be asked questions on what you have studied at A level.

▸ Any extra reading of scientific journals and knowledge about science issues in the news would go down well with interviewers.

▸ Try to find out about the practical applications of chemistry, such as food science or the pharmaceutical industry.

▸ Cogent is the Sector Skills Council for the chemicals and pharmaceuticals, oil and gas, petroleum and polymer industries. Visit: **www.cogent-ssc.com**

▸ Visit: **www.rsc.org** and **www.icheme.org**

Sample interview questions (some of these relate to four-year MSc courses)

General and Mathematical

▸ What have you read recently?

- Why do you want to study chemistry?
- What is your favourite topic in Chemistry? Why do you like it?
- What kind of career are you considering after finishing your Chemistry degree?
- Why did you choose the MSc Chemistry with Industrial Experience?
- How does Chemical Engineering differ from Chemistry?
- You are applying to do Chemical Engineering, but why didn't you consider doing Physics A level?
- What is the most recent Chemistry experiment you have carried out? Describe it.
- What is a recent chemistry innovation that you have read about (excluding graphene!).
- Draw the graph $y = e^{-x^2}$. By differentiation, calculate the turning points.
- What causes the hot and cold seasons on Earth?
- Why is Earth getting warmer?
- Why are the sea levels rising?
- What is gravity?
- What do you know about global warming?

Physical Chemistry

- Draw some half-cells and discuss redox equilibria.
- How can you tell that sodium chloride is bonded ionically?
- What is a covalent bond?
- What does low pH mean?
- Compare the bonding in N_2 to P_4.
- Compare bonding in NaCl (common salt) to diamond.
- Use a phase diagram to understand how changing conditions induce state changes in water.
- Discuss why water's phase diagram differs from other liquids.
- What is the measure of acid strength?
- How many molecules are there in this glass of water?
- NaCl has a cubic structure with a spacing of 0.24nm between each ion. Use this to calculate an estimate for its density.
- Assuming that carbon is 99% ^{12}C and hydrogen is 99.99% 1H, what is the probability that a molecule of C_nH_{2n+2} has exactly K ^{12}C atoms and L 1H atoms?
- If you didn't have an indicator, how can you test the pH and equivalence point of a titration?
- What is the importance of chirality in Chemistry?
- Discuss the properties and applications of graphene.
- Why is methane combusted directly, rather than converted to hydrogen and burnt?
- What do you know about NMR (nuclear magnetic resonance) spectroscopy? What is it that indicates the structure of the compound?
- Explain spin–spin splitting in proton NMR.
- How many different proton environments are there in ethyl ethanoate?
- Roughly where would the peak in an IR spectrum be for an ester group?
- Name the chemical test used to distinguish ketones and aldehydes, explaining how it works.
- How would you tell the difference between butanone and butanal on: NMR spectra, IR spectra and Mass spectra?
- How does IR spectroscopy work?
- Explain the magnetic properties of the transition metals.
- Draw the structure of water and talk about its shape.
- What is eutropy?
- Discuss entropy and enthalpy and their link to the Gibbs free energy.

- The Gas Law states that pV = nRT. How does changing volume affect a gas?
- Draw a volume vs. pressure graph.
- Would an egg cook quicker at sea level or on a mountain?
- How would you identify an ionic compound?
- How would the velocity of sodium ions change when electrolysing brine?
- Explain the relationship between pKa and pH.
- Explain the region on a pH curve where no change in pH is seen, even though volume increases.

Inorganic Chemistry
- Why is sodium chloride soluble in water and barium sulphate insoluble?
- What is special about transition metal compounds?
- Why is copper sulphate blue?
- Predict what would be seen when zinc is added to copper sulphate solution.
- Compare Fluorine's compounds to Caesium's compounds.
- What nitrogen oxides do you know? Explain the structure of nitrogen monoxide and explain the significance of its unpaired electron.

Organic Chemistry
- A chemist wants you to produce C_3H_8O from reactants A and B. Name three structural isomers with this formula.
- Draw and name these three isomers of C_3H_8O.
- The chemist only wants you to produce propan-1-ol; how would you achieve this when the two other chemicals are present?
- What do you get if you react benzene with chlorine?
- How do you know that carbon forms tetrahedral structures?
- What reactions do halogenoalkanes undergo and why?
- Draw propanone. Show its reactions with H^+/OH^-.
- Compare acid chlorides and amides.
- What are the mechanisms for nucleophilic substitution?
- Draw the reaction of bromine and benzene.
- What catalyst would you use to split up bromine?
- Explain a mechanism for esterification.
- Draw the mechanism for carboxyl reacting with NH_2R.

Students' comments

- *'I was asked lots of A level chemistry questions, which I hadn't expected at all.'*
- *'Both my interviews were subject based. One was organic and the other physical and inorganic. I was asked to discuss a topic of my choice and they developed it from there. The questions asked were quite demanding because they wanted you to answer in depth. They didn't want plain facts – they wanted you to think why things happen, apply your existing knowledge and predict reactions you hadn't come across before.'*
- *'I was told I would have an offer when asked for interview. I was given an offer lower than standard advertised with handwritten note at bottom of letter from admissions tutor saying how much he looked forward to seeing him in the new academic year!'*

▶ Classics/Classical Studies/ Classical Civilisation

Essential A levels: For some classics courses, Latin or ancient Greek are required (you may have to translate some text at interview).

Useful A levels (possibly): Classical Civilisation, English Literature and History.

Chance of being interviewed: You should presume that you will get some interviews.

What you need to know

▶ For a classics degree, you will normally be required to have an A level in Latin or Ancient Greek. For Classical Studies or Classical Civilisation, however, most A levels would be considered.

▶ If not ancient Greek or Latin, some flair for languages will definitely help with this course. Some institutions will provide opportunities for you to pick up Latin and/or Greek.

▶ The course covers Literature, Drama, History, Politics and Philosophy. It is suitable for students who enjoy reading books and thinking about the ideas behind them.

▶ Try to visit museums with relevant collections and ancient sites (in Rome or Greece if possible!).

▶ Interview questions will often relate to what you have studied already, especially if you have studied Ancient Greek, Latin or classical civilisation. Most other questioning will tend to refer to what you have put in your personal statement.

▶ If the course involves Latin or Greek literature you may be given a passage and some questions to read through just before the interview.

▶ If you are being interviewed for a course including classical archaeology and ancient history you may be asked to examine and discuss an ancient artefact such as a coin or pot or even a picture.

▶ Visit: **www.classicspage.com**

Sample interview questions

▶ History is a large part of a classics degree, so why aren't you studying it at A level?
▶ Why are you interested in classical archaeology?

▶ What do you think are the differences (if any) between Roman and Greek drama?
▶ What are the similarities between Homer and Virgil?
▶ What have you learned from the dialogues of Plato?
▶ Is Epicurus misunderstood?
▶ How has Greek tragedy influenced modern literature? Give me some examples.
▶ If, as you say, Aristotle has influenced empirical philosophers, in what ways has this occurred?
▶ How is the human body represented in classical art?
▶ Of the things you have studied in your Classical Civilisations A level, what has influenced a modern play, film or novel that you have enjoyed?

Student's comment

▶ *'I was given a test where I had to translate a made-up language.'*

▸ Community and Youth Studies

What you need to know

▸ *See sample interview questions under:* '**Education**', '**Professions allied to Medicine**', '**Sociology**' and '**Social work**'.

▸ Relevant experience or voluntary work will be important.

▸ Visit the website for the Sector Skills Council for care and development: **www.skillsforcare.org.uk**

▸ Visit: **www.csv.org.uk**

▸ Computer courses

Essential A levels: Some courses require Maths. A very small number of courses like Further Maths.

Useful A levels (possibly): Maths, Computing, Physics, Philosophy and ICT.

Chance of being interviewed: You should presume that you will get some interviews, possibly including a test.

What you need to know

▸ Computing degrees vary in their content. Make sure you know exactly what you have applied for as there is a wide range of courses on offer. Some traditional computing courses will involve you in a high level of intellectual questioning while some of the newer courses such as Digital Media will ask you questions to establish that you understand what you are applying for.

▸ Some courses will be very concerned about your maths ability. For others this will be less of an issue. Some courses may be interested in your design ideas. Maths is a strong component in some of the top universities.

▸ Try to think about all the experience you have had with computers and programming, inside and outside of school. Also, think about any work experience that may have involved computer systems. What did you learn from this? Did you have any ideas for improvement?

▸ Visit: **www.bcs.org** and **www.e-skills.com**

Sample interview questions

▸ What is in a computer?

▸ What interests you about computer science? How did you become interested in computers?

▸ What did you do for your A level computer science project?

▸ Why haven't you done computer science up to now? How do you know you will like it?

▸ How would you find the smallest number in a list?

▸ How many zeros are there in 25! (i.e. factorial twenty-five)?

▸ How many zeros are there in 1000! (i.e. factorial one thousand)?

▸ Look at this set of data [provided by interviewer]. What is the minimal spanning tree?

▸ Suggest a method of listing prime numbers to 1000.

- Can machines make their own decisions?
- Express 1 x 109 seconds in a more reliable time frame and proof.

- Integrate $\int_0^2 1/(1-x)^2$ and plot the graph.
- If you have an alphabetically ordered list of names, what is the most efficient method to insert a new name into the correct position in the list, and how many times would the list have to be searched? (no. of items in list = n)
- If you then have X names to be placed in order in an empty list, how many searches have to be performed on the ordered list?
- What programming languages do you know? (from personal statement)
- Which is your favourite? (from personal statement)
- How did you make your games? (from personal statement)
- What did your work experience at Imperial involve? (from personal statement)
- What are the differences in web and application development? (from personal statement)
- Differentiate $y=x^x$.
- If an ant is on a corner of a cube, what is the easiest way for it to get to the opposite corner?

Here are some questions from the Oxford University Computer Lab, Copyright © 2004-8 J.M. Spivey:

- *Tidy boxes.* You are given ten boxes, each large enough to contain exactly ten wooden building blocks, and a total of 100 blocks in ten different colours. There may not be the same number in each colour, so you may not be able to pack the blocks into the boxes in such a way that each box contains only one colour of block. Show that it is possible to do it so that each box contains at most two different colours.

- *Searching for the maximum.* The real-valued function $f(x)$, defined for $0 \leq x \leq 1$, has a single maximum at $x = m$. If $0 \leq u < v \leq m$ then $f(u) < f(v)$, and if $m \leq u < v \leq 1$ then $f(u) > f(v)$. You are told nothing else about f, but you may ask for the value of $f(x)$ for any values of x you choose. How would you find the approximate value of m? How accurately could you find m if you could choose only ten values of x for which to evaluate $f(x)$?

- *Death by chocolate.* You are locked in a room with your worst enemy. On a table in the centre of the room is a bar of chocolate, divided into squares in the usual way. One square of the chocolate is painted with a bright green paint that contains a deadly nerve poison. You and your enemy take it in turns to break off one or more squares from the remaining chocolate (along a straight line) and eat them. Whoever is left with the green square must eat it and die in agony. You may look at the bar of chocolate and then decide whether to go first or second. Describe your strategy.

- *Monkey beans.* An urn contains twenty-three white beans and thirty-four black beans. A monkey takes out two beans; if they are the same, he puts a black bean into the urn, and if they are different, he puts in a white bean from a large heap he has next to him. The monkey repeats this procedure until there is only one bean left. What colour is it?

- *Lily-pad lunacy.* Eleven lily pads are numbered from 0 to 10. A frog starts on pad 0 and wants to get to pad 10. At each jump, the frog can move forward by one or two pads, so there are many ways it can get to pad ten. For example, it can make ten jumps of one pad, 1111111111, or five jumps of two pads, 22222, or go 221212 or 221122, and so on. We'll call each of these ways different, even if the frog takes the same jumps in a different order. How many different ways are there of getting from 0 to 10?

- *Missing numbers.* Imagine you are given a list of slightly less than 1,000,000 numbers, all different, and each from 0 to 999,999. How could you find (in a reasonable time) a number from 0 to 999,999 that is not on the list?

▸ Scribble. The game of *Scribble* is played with an inexhaustible supply of tiles, and consists of forming 'words' according to certain rules. Since each tile bears one of the letters **P**, **Q**, or **R**, these are not words that will be found in an ordinary dictionary. The game begins with the word **PQ** on the board; each move consists of applying one of the following rules:

  – If the word on the board is **P***x*, for some shorter word *x*, you may change it to **P***xx*. For example, if the word is **PQRRQ** then you may change it to **PQRRQQRRQ**.

  – If the word on the board is *x***QQQ***y*, for some shorter words *x* and *y*, then you may change it to *x***R***y*, replacing the sequence **QQQ** with a single **R**.

  – If the word on the board is *x***RR***y*, for some shorter words *x* and *y*, then you may change it to *xy*, deleting the sequence **RR** entirely.

  (i) For each of the following words, say whether you can make it or not by following the rules of the game: **QPR**, **PQQ**, **PQR**, **PR**.

  (ii) Given any word, how can you decide whether it can be made or not?

Some general hints:

▸ If the problem contains specific numbers (like 10, 100, 23, 34), does it become easier if we replace those numbers with smaller ones, or even by 0 or 1 or 2? If there are no specific numbers, can you solve the problem in small examples, such as a 2 x 1 bar of chocolate?

▸ Are there other simplifying assumptions that you can try? What if the bar of chocolate consists of just one row of squares? What if the green square is in one corner?

▸ Is there a way of reducing the problem as given to a smaller one? Is there a way of filling the first box of blocks that eliminates a colour, leaving us with nine boxes and nine colours?

▸ Some of these problems have definitive answers, others do not – or not answers that can be reached during a half-hour conversation, anyway. Most of them can be solved in several stages, beginning with easy cases and getting more general; some problems can be generalised beyond what is asked in the question.

Students' comments

▸ *'After a preliminary conversation and questioning, I was asked to solve some problems on paper. As soon as each problem was on paper they expected the solution – impatience was in the air, as was an unforgiving demand for accuracy. I'm afraid I cracked under the pressure. Applicants should be aware that the nature of pressure changes very much when one has to write, rather than talk.'*

▸ *'A lot of the interview seemed to be based on the question, "Why did you apply for this course?" It would seem the stock response is, "Because I like computers." So a better answer to this question would probably be about why computers are important.'*

▸ *'No personal questions so found it difficult to demonstrate my passions. Interviews were problem-focused and impersonal.'*

▸ *'I had one interview with a computer professor and one with a physics/maths specialist.'*

▶ Criminology

See sample interview questions under: **'Sociology', 'Law'** *and* **'Psychology'**.

▶ Dance

What you need to know

▶ Prepare well for auditions and take account of the differing procedures at the various schools of dance that you have applied to.

▶ Make sure you know whether or not the courses you are applying for will train you as a professional dancer.

▶ Look at the sample interview questions under: **'Drama and Theatre Studies'**.

▶ Visit: www.cdet.org.uk

▶ Dentistry

Essential A levels: Chemistry and Biology would be acceptable for most courses, but a few still prefer Chemistry, Biology and Maths or Physics.

Chance of being interviewed: See also **'Applying for Medicine'** chapter as many of the processes used are similar if your application passes the initial selection. Increasingly, Multiple Mini Interviews (MMIs) are used. Like Medicine, ethical issues are featuring more prominently in selections interviews. Look at other examples in the Medicine chapter and under Veterinary Science.

What you need to know

▶ You will need to be able to explain fully why you want to become a dentist and provide evidence to back up your claims. How would you cope with the pressure of the course?

▶ Interviewers will be interested in any work experience you have done in dentistry. Can you explain what you learned from it?

▶ Show your interest by being aware of some current issues or difficulties facing dentists. Is there one that you could talk about in more depth?

▶ Interviewers will want to know that you have a high level of manual dexterity. Try to think of things you have done that prove your manual dexterity. Some courses require you to undertake a manual dexterity test.

▶ Most dental schools will require you to take the UKCAT: www.ukcat.ac.uk

▶ Visit the websites of the British Dental Association (www.bda.org) and the General Dental Council (www.gdc-uk.org).

▶ For dental hygiene/oral health, visit: www.bsdht.org.uk

Sample interview questions

▸ Why do you want to do dentistry, rather than medicine?

▸ How come you want to do dentistry when you are not doing biology A level?

▸ What would you like to do after your dentistry degree, for example: research, a BSc or general practice?

▸ What skills and qualities make a good dentist? Give some examples.

▸ How do you know that you are manually dexterous?

▸ How do you help a friend if they are anxious?

▸ What would you *not* like about dentistry?

▸ What are orthodontics?

▸ What is cosmetic dentistry?

▸ What is preventative dentistry?

▸ Tell us what you know about tooth decay.

▸ Do you know of any current issues or difficulties facing dentists today? Tell us more about one particular issue.

▸ Where do you see dentistry going in the future?

▸ What do you know about the oral health of your age group?

▸ Do you think that a degree in dentistry is about training or education?

▸ What is meant by 'to be a member of a profession'?

▸ What do you know about the General Dental Council?

▸ How is NHS dentistry controlled? Why?

▸ What noticeable differences do you see between NHS and private?

▸ What would it be like if there was only private dentistry?

▸ What are your negative qualities? What are your strengths?

▸ What was the most important thing you learned from your work experience?

▸ Tell us about your work experience.

▸ Tell us how you have shown team work.

▸ What volunteering have you done?

▸ What are your hobbies?

▸ What are you reading?

▸ What is hepatitis A? B?

▸ Why do dentists needs immunising?

▸ What are controversial issues in dentistry?

▸ Where do you see yourself in ten years?

▸ How do you cope with stress? Do you think you will be able to cope with the pressure?

▸ Scenario: If a teacher was not paying that much attention to you and your class, what would you do?

▸ Given a picture and asked to describe it. Why do you think we have asked you to describe it?

▸ Just before interview, I was shown a DVD of an interaction between dentist and patient. I was asked questions based on the DVD:
  – What are the ethical issues involved in this case?
  – How would you rate the dentist's performance?
  – What problems can you see?

Students' comments

▸ *'I came away feeling that it was an unfair interview, but in fact I was only questioned about things I had put in UCAS Apply (though in a very challenging manner). Nothing really was asked about dentistry.'*

▸ *'It was very important to know what you had gained from your work experience – sort of, "What is life like beside the dentist's chair?"!'*

▸ *'I was given ethical scenario before interview. Part of interview was based on scenario was MMI format with 5 stations. 5 minutes per station with a 90 second gap between stations.'*

▸ *'The dental school used MMIs. I thought this was fairer than a standard interview as I had 5 chances to show what I could do. Each station lasted for 5 minutes and discussions ranged from work experience to an ethical dilemma.'*

▸ Development Studies

See sample interview questions under: **'Economics', 'Geography', 'Politics', 'Sociology'** *and* **'Anthropology'.**

▸ Dietetics

See sample interview questions under: **'Professions Allied to Medicine'.**

▸ Drama and Theatre Studies

Essential A levels: Some courses require English literature. A few courses specify English and theatre studies.

Useful A levels (possibly): English Literature, English Literature and Language and Theatre Studies.

Chance of being interviewed: Expect to be called for an interview and audition from all of your choices. Drama and Theatre Studies courses vary enormously depending on the focus of the particular course. Interviews/auditions, not uncommonly, last 1–2 days and involve group activities, workshops, acting, mini productions and seek to examine both talent and team work. Assessors sit in on the various components and score the candidates.

What you need to know

▸ If you want to enter a career in professional acting, you will find essential information on **www.dramauk.co.uk** (**www.ncdt.co.uk**). You need to be clear about which courses will train you to work as a professional actor and which courses are more concerned with the criticism and analysis of the theatre.

▸ Check whether the drama schools you are interested in handle their own applications or work through UCAS. If you need to apply directly to the school do so well before the deadline (varies).

▸ Check on the schools' individual websites whether bursaries or scholarships are available.

▸ If you are applying for acting courses, be clear about what you have learned from all the roles you have played so far.

▸ If you are applying for technical courses, think about the problems you have encountered in the productions you have been involved with and how you have dealt with those problems.

▸ Seek advice from teachers or tutors with recent and successful experience of helping people prepare for audition.

▸ For an honest idea of the industry see: **www.equity.org.uk**

▸ Each initial audition will cost about £35 to £60. There is no charge if you are called back for further auditions.

▸ The Sector Skills Councils for acting are Creative and Cultural: **www.ccskills.org.uk** and Skillset: **www.creativeskillset.org**

▸ The process varies considerably across different institutions (see Students' comments). The different approaches reflect the different emphases of the courses.

Sample interview questions

▸ What do you like about the course?
▸ What would you bring to the course?
▸ Tell us about yourself. Why do you want to do Drama?
▸ Which modern playwrights do you like?
▸ Talk about the last play you saw.
▸ What books do you like to read?
▸ In what ways would an actor benefit from learning to dance?
▸ Talk about Shakespeare as a dramatist.
▸ Tell us about the qualities you like in an actor you admire.

▸ What is the most memorable performance you have seen?
▸ What role does theatre play in society today?

▸ What would you do if you did not get into university?
▸ Do you think that the university publicising its students in a book to the industry is a good idea?

▸ Why do you think Willy Russell wrote 'Blood Brothers'? (in response to memorable performance question).
▸ How do you think the statement 'The Death of the Author' applies to plays as well as books?

▸ Have you seen any theatre productions recently?
▸ How would you stage a novel?

▸ Explain and talk us through what you've brought with you (based on portfolio taken).
▸ What other careers have you looked at?

▸ How did you get into Theatre Design? What interests you about Theatre Design?

▸ Explain what could be improved about your work (based on portfolio taken).
▸ What discipline are you most interested in?

▸ What type of dance are you interested in?
▸ What dance experience have you had (i.e. lessons, performances)?
▸ What do you hope to do as a career after this course?

Students' comments

▶ 'It was not an interview, it was an audition. I had to learn three pieces to perform, of no more than two minutes each: some Shakespeare in blank verse; a contemporary work; and something of my own choice.'

▶ 'As well as the interview there was a 45-minute drama practical, which included mime and speech, individual and pair work. I didn't find it too difficult.'

▶ 'I had a 2 hour workshop with approximately 20 other people interpreting a play and playing "games" and improvisation.'

▶ 'Start looking for your monologues in Year 12. Most drama schools ask to see an Elizabethan or Jacobean piece. Shakespeare tends to be a good choice but you must choose a monologue that lasts roughly two minutes. The other monologue should be from a modern play. Also, prepare a back-up monologue. Check the websites or prospectuses because some have specific requirements – some even give a list of suggested audition pieces. Give yourself at least a few months to prepare and perform your pieces in front of as many people and as many times as you can.'

▶ 'I had a group interview with approx. 50 students together at first and then split into 16/17.'

▶ 'I had to do a role play from a piece of pre-sent prose.'

▶ 'I had to submit an additional application form online. There were multiple-choice questions to ascertain my interests and I had 200 words on a piece of theatre that had inspired me with a critique of a performance. I then had a 20 minute interview and was asked about what my approach would be to directing a piece from scratch with no text to follow.'

▶ 'I was invited to a half day workshop in groups of about 15 students. We took it in turn to discuss themes on a recent piece of theatre we had seen and were given tasks around it / interaction. We were then split into smaller groups and had to devise a short performance based on a text sent a few weeks before.'

▶ 'Vocal workshop – asked to prepare 30 second improvisation with 2 others using only sounds and movement (no words).'

▶ 'Groups of 10-15 – given 1 hour to create a 2 minute improvisation on choice of themes.'

▶ 'It's essential to arrive early for your dance audition so that you have plenty of time to warm up. Some dancers arrived late and got in a panic about changing and warming up.'

▶ 'When it came to the actual dance audition the panel made people wearing legwarmers take them off – but they didn't ask nicely at all. Being shouted at in front of a group of people you don't know is very unnerving!'

▶ Economics

Essential A levels: Most courses specify Maths.

Useful A levels (possibly): Maths and Economics.

Chance of being interviewed: Most courses will make offers on the basis what is in UCAS Apply, but a small number of courses still interview all applicants.

What you need to know

▶ Keep abreast of economic issues that are in the news.

▶ If you are studying economics at A level, be prepared to talk in depth about topics you have covered.

▸ If you are not studying economics at A level, be prepared to do some extra reading on some economic issues that interest you. Also, think about the A levels you are taking to see if they have any cross-curricular links with economics. Be prepared to talk about these.

▸ It is important to show that you have a genuine interest in economics – not just an interest in working for an investment bank!

▸ Visit: **www.res.org.uk** and the Financial Skills Partnership: **www.financialskillspartnership.org.uk** and **www.directions.org.uk**

Sample interview questions

▸ Is economics a science?

▸ How is inflation caused?

▸ Why do we have low inflation?

▸ What would you do to solve a country's long-term inflation problems?

▸ What has been the affect of the minimum wage on the economy?

▸ If a high minimum wage leads to unemployment, would you still support it?

▸ What indirect taxes would you impose?

▸ Is the current British taxation system fair? What effect do tax thresholds have? What is meant by 'the poverty trap'?

▸ What do you think about the inequality of earning in society? Is it right for people of higher natural intelligence to earn more money?

▸ Discuss interest rate movements and their effects on the strength of a currency, imports/exports and investment.

▸ What is wrong with having a balance of payments deficit? Can't a surplus be just as bad?

▸ What do you think about the privatisation of public utilities and the oligopolies it has created?

▸ If private companies who have won infrastructure contracts always overrun in time and cost, why does the government still contract out?

▸ How would you distinguish between a 'recession' and a 'depression'?

▸ What do you understand by the term 'securitisation'?

▸ How important are economic models?

▸ What is monetarism? Who started it?

▸ How does monetary policy affect bond prices?

▸ What are the differences between Keynes and Friedman?

▸ Work out, on a whiteboard, the principle of supply and demand, starting from first principles.

▸ In economics, what is the multiplier?

▸ What are push and pull factors?

▸ What will push someone away from a country? What is the affect on the country?

▸ Give examples of pull factors and explain the affect on the country of increased immigration.

▸ What is de-materialisation?

▸ Give an example of a product that uses de-materialisation.

▸ In what ways can de-materialisation relate to consumption of materials?

▸ Give an example of a positive externality.

▸ How has globalisation affected the economy?

▸ What stories have you been following lately in *The Economist*?

▸ Do you think that *The Economist* has a political standpoint and, if so, which one?

▸ Discuss any major current economic problem or issue.

- Should we let Greece leave the Euro? What are the pros/cons?
- Are banks too big to fail? Should the government intervene? How?

- What are the pros and cons of the European Monetary Union (EMU)?
- Discuss the European Union's (EU's) agricultural policy. How does it work and who does it benefit? How has it affected countries outside the EU?
- When the countries of Eastern Europe joined the European Union, what were thought to be the disadvantages?
- In terms of world trade, what are the benefits for a country of being in a trade bloc?
- What are tradeable pollution permits? Are they effective?

- What can be done to reduce pollution in the world, particularly in developing countries?
- Compare the effects of an earthquake in San Francisco and one in a developing country.
- Should we encourage nuclear power?
- What are the problems facing agriculture in Britain?
- What economic affect would a peace settlement in the Middle East have?
- Find the elasticity of a demand function: $\log q = a + b \log p$ $q = a + bp$.
- 25 minutes to look at unseen material
  - Henry Ford's policy to raise wages to double going rate. How would this increase profits? Would policy need to be introduced to both existing and new workers, or just new? Would success of policy have been undermined if others had done the same?
- (Most of interview) A bank has £100 to lend to a borrower who will invest it in a risky project. 50% of the time the outcome will be £101 + X, where $X > 1$, and the borrower will then pay R in interest. The other 50% of the time they will make a loss, £101 − X, and will simply pay the bank what they have left as compensation. In this situation, what is the minimum interest rate the bank will be prepared to accept and what is the maximum interest rate that the borrower will be prepared to pay if the bank wants to get back at least £100?
  - Half of borrowers are good and half bad. 50% of the time good borrowers will have the outcome £101 + X_g and the other 50% of the time it will be £101 − X_g. For bad borrowers, 50% of the time it will be £101 + X_b and the other 50% of the time £101 − X_b. $X_b > X_g$. Borrowers know whether they are good or bad, but banks cannot distinguish between the two. How will this affect answers to the previous questions?

Students' comments

- *'It's important to be up-to-date with current affairs and to have an opinion. You also need to know about all the relevant books, journals and newspapers and be aware of their political stances.'*
- *'I was asked to choose a mathematical technique or theorem (such as induction or dimensional analysis) and explain the process. Then the interviewer asked me to apply that technique to economics. It was a very unusual interview.'*
- *'Most of the interview was taken up with questions on maths and statistics which the interviewer set out for me. I had to do the equations on a board in front of him.'*
- *'Given 2 articles on micro-economics. Asked to draw 6 graphs. Questioned on both articles and graphs. Discussion about economic spending, cuts, etc.'*
- *'Maths questions included equations, drawing graphs and explaining them.'*

▸ Education (Teacher Training)

Essential A levels: At least one from: Art, Biology, Chemistry, Design and Technology, Drama (Theatre Studies), English, French, Geography, German, History, ICT, Italian, Maths, Music, Physical Education, Physics, Religious Studies (Theology), Spanish. Courses such as CACHE and BTEC Level 3 Extended Diploma Health and Social Care are often considered for General Primary Education degrees (although it should be noted that these students are increasingly in competition with standard A level applicants with increasingly high grades).

Chance of being interviewed: It is a requirement that all applicants for teacher training are interviewed.

What you need to know

▸ Primary Education applicants need to adopt the same meticulous attitude as medicine applicants – competition for places is now fierce; 'failing to prepare is preparing to fail'

▸ At interview you are normally asked to provide a short written statement on a given topic to ascertain your standard of written English

▸ Make sure you read all the instructions/notes/details sent to you before your interview in depth. Do you understand what is being expected of you on the day?

▸ All trainee teachers are required to pass skills tests in numeracy and literacy before they can be recommended for the award of qualified teacher status (QTS). Applicants to initial teacher training (ITT) courses that start after 1 July 2013 will be required to pass the skills tests before starting their course

▸ You must have had some sort of work experience or observational experience in a school appropriate to the age range for which you are applying. You will almost certainly be asked to comment/reflect on these. Keep a diary of what you observed, learned, found challenging and interesting

▸ You must have English, maths and science GCSE at grade C or above to teach in state primary education

▸ You must do more than just describe your experience. What did you learn from it? What difficulties did the teachers face? What did they enjoy about the job? What initiatives were being implemented? Did you think there was too much testing? What made a teacher a good teacher?

▸ Is there an academic discipline you want to specialise in? If not, why not?

▸ You should expect to be with the university for about 4 hours and maybe longer and you may be submitted to a wide range of testing including:
  – A written reflective task
  – Creating a lesson plan from suggested stimuli
  – A test of systematic synthetic phonics
  – Mental maths
  – A short science test
  – An individual interview
  – A small group presentation based on a topic given, book, artefact that you have brought in or a dvd that is shown
  – Your ability to respond to questions asked by fellow applicants

▸ Visit Professional Skills Test:
www.education.gov.uk/schools/careers/traininganddevelopment/professional

▸ **www.education.gov.uk/get-into-teaching**

Sample interview questions

▸ Why do you want to become a teacher?

▸ What is a teacher's role?

▸ What kind of qualities should a teacher have? Give an example of a good teacher. Why was he/she good?

▸ What, in your opinion and from your own experience, makes a bad teacher?

▸ Tell us about a teacher you admire, and why.

▸ Describe an inspirational teacher.

▸ What are your own good qualities and how are they relevant to teaching?

▸ What qualities does a teacher need?

▸ What actually is a 'good' teacher?

▸ What are your views on current issues in the news regarding education?

▸ Which teaching techniques do you think are important?

▸ How do you manage your time with your workload?

▸ What is your weakest subject at school?

▸ What experience of children have you had? Do you have experience of working with children?

▸ How is your work experience relevant to teaching? What has it taught you?

▸ What additional skills do you have that would be of benefit to a career in teaching (e.g. drama, sports)?

▸ What difficulties might you come across as a teacher?

▸ Tell us about a time when you have helped a child.

▸ What do you think about the National Curriculum?

▸ What do you think about recent changes in the education system?

▸ Have you had any experiences of special methods of teaching Maths?

▸ Talk about the use of technology in the classroom.

▸ How important is RE in the National Curriculum?

▸ What are the features of an inclusive classroom?

▸ Is gender important for primary teachers?

▸ Should modern foreign languages be in the primary school curriculum?

▸ Is healthy eating important in primary schools?

▸ Global warming – should it be taught in primary schools?

▸ How would you relate to other members of staff at school? What skills would you need?

▸ How would you deal with prejudices in the classroom?

▸ Do you think you will be able to develop good relationships with parents? How?

▸ 'Sell' a recent book you have read.

▸ Why is PE important in schools? How are the skills gained from PE important later in life?

▸ How important are control of obesity and PE lessons in school?

▸ What is the importance of teaching history in schools? In what ways can history be taught to children?

▸ Why do you want to specialise in teaching the youngest age group?

▸ Why do you particularly want to teach children with learning difficulties?

▸ Why do you need a CRB/DBS check and what is it?

Students' comments

▸ *'We had a group interview – pre-set questions were sent in advance through the post. On the day we had to choose one question for group discussion.'*

▸ *'It was a very well-structured day. It started with a 45-minute talk about the course. Then we had to write an essay with the title, "Who is a teacher accountable to?" They said it didn't matter so much what we wrote – they were more interested in style and accuracy. Then we were interviewed individually by a local head teacher and a lecturer from the university.'*

▸ *'I applied to specialise in English and drama. The first part of the day was a session of practical exercises in drama techniques. Then we were put into groups of six and had to do a critical analysis of some poetry. Finally, there was a personal interview.'*

▸ *'The practical PE assessment was very tiring and physically demanding. It included running, ball skills, gymnastics (forward and backward rolls, handstand, cartwheel) and a short dance sequence.'*

▸ *'I applied to specialise in history and they expected me to have a lot of knowledge. I was asked to identify some historical artefacts. Then they asked me how I would explain them to children and how they could be used for further work.'*

▸ *'I was given a poem to discuss in a group.'*

▸ *'I had to choose an object from a range and give a 2 minute presentation on how I would use it in the classroom.'*

▸ *'There was a written test. I had to choose a book that I would use to teach children, explain why I would use it and how I would use it in the classroom.'*

▸ *'We were split into groups of four. We had to choose a topic from a set of cards (the topics included school dinners, languages and SATs). We then had to choose one of these topics and make a group presentation which was observed.'*

▸ *'There was a written task – to write a 300 word response to 'How can a teacher promote effective learning?''*

▸ *'There was a group task – discussion and presentation on how could a teacher use the book 'Where the wild things are' in a lesson.'*

▸ *'The morning tasks involved writing a written essay on why you want to be a primary school teacher and then we had to make a verbal presentation on an artefact/book on an aspect of the national curriculum. If we were successful in this, we then proceeded to the afternoon task which was a 1:1 interview.'*

▸ *'Asked, in advance, to prepare a 5 minute teaching task on topic of own choice. Plus an English essay on choice of 6 topics – "An event/day most memorable to you" chosen.'*

▸ *'There was no formal interview. We were shown a 10 minute film of a lesson and asked to make notes on: styles of teaching, techniques, discipline, and health & safety in classroom. We were then split into groups of 5 or 6 where we were observed discussing the film clip. The next task involved speaking for two minutes on a topic that we had chosen from a list sent to us before the interview, then each candidate in the group had to think of a question to ask the other candidates, then you had answer one of these questions. We were marked on listening skills and ability to respond to others.'*

▸ *'We were asked to plan a lesson of our choice and consider how we would take into account the different learning preferences created by the individual needs of a range of children.'*

▸ Engineering

See also 'Chemistry/Chemical Engineering'.

Essential A levels: Maths and Physics (Chemistry for Chemical Engineering).

Useful A levels (possibly): Further Maths and Design and Technology.

Chance of being interviewed: Many courses do still interview.

What you need to know

▸ Make sure you know whether the courses that you are applying for will lead to you becoming a chartered or an incorporated engineer.

▸ If you are applying for a general engineering degree, you will need to be able to explain why. If you are applying for a more specialist engineering degree (for example, civil engineering), again, why?

▸ Look at the world around you. Do you see examples of engineering that fascinate you? Why do they fascinate you? How do they look? How were they made? What elements of Maths and Physics were used?

▸ Be aware of programmes such as 'A Year in Industry' and Headstart: **www.etrust.org.uk**

▸ Visit the websites of the professional bodies listed here:

Royal Academy of Engineering: **www.raeng.org.uk**
Institution of Civil Engineers: **www.ice.org.uk**
Institution of Chemical Engineers: **www.icheme.org** Also see Internet sources for Chemistry.
Institution of Engineering and Technology (Electrical and Electronic): **www.theiet.org**
Institution of Mechanical Engineers: **www.imeche.org**
The Royal Aeronautical Society: **www.aerosociety.com**
The Institute of Electrical and Electronic Engineers: **www.ieee-ukri.org**

Sample interview questions

▸ What do you think engineering is?
▸ Give a dictionary definition of engineering.
▸ Where does your interest in engineering stem from?
▸ What interests you about Mechanical Engineering?
▸ What aspect of electronics are you interested in?
▸ How do you see the relationship between electronics and mathematics?
▸ What is the difference between a civil engineer and an architect?
▸ Why do you want to do aeronautics?
▸ What do you understand by the word 'acoustics'?

▸ Have you had any experience of industry? Do you know anyone who works in industry?
▸ Have you thought about getting sponsorship?

▸ Can you explain the physics principles in Newton's third law? (Density, etc.)
▸ Consider a car accelerating up a hill. Describe all the external forces.

▸ How would you calculate acceleration? Apart from F=ma, give another way of writing Newton's second law.

▸ What is charge?

▸ Define simple harmonic motion, giving equations.

▸ Prove the area of a triangle is 1/2b x h.

▸ Calculate from first principles, the maximum force a suction machine can generate.

▸ Describe an experiment you have done in physics. Where have you used what you learned from this experiment?

▸ Tell us about your GCSE technology project (from personal statement).

▸ Describe the aerodynamics and electronics you designed for your GCSE technology project.

▸ What work have you done on computers and what programs have you written?

▸ What hobbies do you have related to engineering?

Students' comments

▸ *'I had a 20 minute aptitude test which was a mixture of lateral thinking, non-verbal reasoning and general knowledge of engineering E.g. Who was Isambard Kingdom Brunel?'*

▸ *'Most of the interview revolved around differential equations when applied to taps filling buckets with water, and questions about capacitors.'*

▸ *'In the computation interview, the interviewer asked me how many questions I would need to ask to find a specific square he had chosen on a chessboard, if he could only answer my questions with yes or no and if the board had 128 squares.'*

▸ *'I was asked specific questions about mechanics, oscillation and magnetic fields.'*

▸ *'Both my interviews were very technical. Most questions somehow related to physics subjects (mechanics, electricity, forces and moments, etc.).'*

▸ English

Essential A levels: English Literature or English Literature and Language.

Useful A levels (possibly): History, Theology/Religious Studies, Classical Civilisation, Modern Foreign Languages, Latin and Ancient Greek.

Chance of being interviewed: Most courses will make offers on the basis of what is in the UCAS Apply, however a significant minority of courses do still interview.

What you need to know

▸ You need to be genuinely enthusiastic about poems, plays and novels, from classical civilisations to the present day.

▸ Reading beyond your A level syllabus is essential. You will need to talk about your favourite authors, poets and dramatists and explain why you like them.

▸ The sample interview questions below give you an idea of the type of questioning you will face. The texts chosen for discussion, however, will tend to be those mentioned by you on your UCAS Apply.

▸ Try to think about issues relating to literature in a wider context, such as the difference between studying a text in depth or reading it for pleasure, and its links with history and religion.

- For background reading look at: *Literary Theory: A Very Short Introduction* by Jonathan Culler and *Beginning Theory: An Introduction to Literary and Cultural Theory (Beginnings)* by Peter Barry.
- Most degrees are literature based so do not go on about creative writing and journalism.
- Poetry forms the basis of many interviews and pre-interview tests.

Sample interview questions

- What book are you reading at the moment? Are you enjoying it and, if so, why?
- What books do you want to talk about?
- What do you read for enjoyment?
- What would you consider literature?
- Is anything literature?
- Can you apply a literary analysis to anything?
- Why study English?
- Are you not angry at the silence of women in literature?
- What do you read other than literature?
- What did you read for AS and A2 English?

- Who is your favourite nineteenth- or twentieth-century novelist?
- What do you think of the character of Fanny Price in Jane Austen's *Mansfield Park*?
- In *Great Expectations* by Charles Dickens, how limiting is the use of the first-person form of narration?
- In *The Return of the Native* by Thomas Hardy, what do you think Egdon Heath represents?
- Do you think novels such as those of Jane Austen should be adapted for the screen?

- Is there any hope in *Nineteen Eighty-four* and *The Handmaid's Tale*? (from personal statement)
- Is *A Clockwork Orange* a dystopian book and about a dystopia? (i.e. can a book be in a genre and about that genre simultaneously?)
- What is Burgess' message and how does he get his message across?
  - What did you like about the book?

- Your personal statement seems to be full of books you read for school; what have you read independently?
- Why did you like Fitzgerald's *Flappers and Philosophers*? (from personal statement)
- Can you give an example of humour in this text?
- Are the stories about failed dislocations according to you?
- Do you like Daisy in *The Great Gatsby*? Why?
- What exactly does Daisy say that makes you dislike her?

- Is there anything about Kafka's language in *Meditations* that reveals something to the reader about the time in which he lived?

- Which of Shakespeare's plays have you read, other than those you have studied at school?
- Did you actually enjoy reading Shakespeare? Why?
- How would you define Shakespearean tragedy?
- What do you think of the ending of *King Lear*?
- How do you think the opening scene of *King Lear* influences the rest of the play?
- What does the interaction between the mad Lear and the disguised Edgar communicate and achieve?
- What should one feel about the character of Macbeth?

▸ Does Lady Macbeth sacrifice herself for Macbeth?

▸ Is it possible to read Macbeth as a romance?

▸ What do you think Shakespeare suggests about the character of Macbeth in the scene in which he hallucinates and thinks he can see a dagger?

▸ What do you consider to be the main theme of *Othello*?

▸ Why does Othello shy away from talking about sex?

▸ Describe the sexual tension in *Much Ado About Nothing*. What does it tell us?

▸ What are the dramatic failures in *Hamlet*?

▸ Why is *Hamlet* longer than *Macbeth*?

▸ Compare *Twelfth Night* to one of the tragedies you have read.

▸ What is the significance of the theme of appearances vs. reality in *Twelfth Night* and *King Lear*?

▸ Can we ever know if reality is ever fully restored after a character reveals their true identity?

▸ What do you make of the ending of *Twelfth Night*, since Viola remains in her brother's clothes as the curtain falls?

▸ What is significant about Lear's slow recognition of Cordelia?

▸ Why was this important for the tragedy? Why would this motif be important for tragedies in general?

▸ What images does Shakespeare use to describe what Gloucester pictures after he supposedly walks off the cliff?

▸ Why is this significant?

▸ Discuss Chaucer's art.

▸ Do you think Chaucer's *The Wife of Bath's Tale* represents women well?

▸ How is *The Wife of Bath's Tale* relevant to today?

▸ Do you think the wife of Bath is a strong character?

▸ Choose a poem you have read and discuss its imagery, sentence structure, tone and meaning.

▸ Recite 'On a Grecian Urn' by Keats and then analyse it.

▸ Discuss some poems from *The Whitsun Weddings* by Philip Larkin.

▸ Analyse the poem 'Harrow-on-the-Hill' by John Betjeman.

▸ Was William Wordsworth patronising towards his sister Dorothy?

▸ What do you think of the poetry in Ben Jonson's play *Volpone*?

▸ What poetry do you read outside of school and why do you enjoy it?

▸ Would you say 'The Flea' and 'The Good Morrow' are love poems? (from personal statement)

▸ 30 minutes prep. time for 3 unseen poems. Choose one of the poems to discuss. What is it about? Why?
  – Why did you find it abstract/ambiguous?
  – Can you find any other examples of liminality?
  – Find the exact word in the poem that tells you that … took place.
  – What does the passive voice symbolise?
  – Is there something humorous?
  – What two phrases relating to the words 'cheques' and 'escalators' respectively imply visiting a bereaved family?
  – Is the poem a funereal ritual or is it about funereal ritual?
  – What is your one final reading of the poem?

▸ What is the relationship between literature and art?

▸ How would you approach translating a text?

▸ Why would a writer bother to write a play when it will inevitably be subject to interpretation from the actors and director?

▸ When does satire become cynicism?

- Discuss the importance of 'context' in literature.
- How is Shakespeare's approach to tragedy different from Aristotle's? Is it different at all?
- How would you interpret Hamlet from a feminist perspective?
- Apply a feminist critique of *Nineteen Eighty-four*.
- What is the importance of feminist criticism? Which feminist critics have you read?
- Apply your criticisms of the feminist perspective to Austen's *Pride and Prejudice*.
- Apply a Marxist perspective to a novel of your choice. Then to the same novel apply a feminist perspective.
- How much of a sociological impact can a piece of literature have?

- Define the words: 'metre', 'ballad', 'phrase', 'genre', 'pronoun'.
- What are the issues with transferring a book to a screenplay?
- What do you know about critics? What is the importance of critics? Can you quote one?
- In this day of Xbox™ and Playstation™ and all the mechanisms vying for our attention, what would be your argument for the importance of literature?

In response to an unseen poem:
- What did you notice about the poem?
- What is interesting about these two words?
- Can you find another word that is similar in the same way?
- What is important about the title? What do you think about the title?
- Is there any part that reminds you of another poem you have read? Why?
- What is the poem about?
- Can you think of an alternative interpretation/meaning?
- Find examples of inversion in the poem.

Students' comments

- 'Having taken a year out, I found it quite difficult to discuss Shakespeare in great detail, especially Macbeth, which I studied for GCSE.'
- 'I had an English test on language not literature.'
- 'I had a test of 1hr on 2 pieces of prose and was asked to discuss the "arrangement of people, space and things" in both texts.'
- 'The interview was based almost wholly on poetry and a good base of knowledge was imperative. It seemed almost like a verbal practical criticism. Every statement I made had to be fully supported.'
- 'Make sure you are thoroughly familiar with the work of at least two poets. It is important to be confident and the only way you will be is if you are familiar with all your texts and a base of poetry.'
- 'I was handed a lengthy poem, told to read it and asked to deliver a practical criticism. This was a bit nerve-racking but I think it is important to take your time to read and absorb the text and form your own opinions.'
- 'It is vital to know your texts well and it is worth preparing a couple of books that aren't on the syllabus for a discussion about your private reading.'
- 'I was asked to read over a poem and then discuss it with the interviewer. Then I was asked to speak for five minutes on a book of my choice (unprepared).'
- 'They are impressed if you use short memorised quotes to illustrate the points you make, especially from the poetry you study.'

▸ *'I would recommend knowing your personal statement and the books it mentions very thoroughly.'*

▸ *'I was given two openings from 19th century novels and I had to explain which opening I thought was most effective.'*

▸ *'Good job I like poetry. It all seemed to be about unseen poems.'*

▸ *'90% of my questions were based on unseen poetry.'*

▸ Environmental Health

See sample interview questions under: **'Professions Allied to Health'**, **'Geography'** *and* **'Biology'**.

What you need to know

▸ Environmental health officers ensure that people are protected from a wide range of hazards in the environment in its widest sense. To find out more, visit the website of the Chartered Institute of Environmental Health: **www.cieh.org**

▸ You will need to be able to explain fully why you want be become an environmental health officer. Can you provide evidence to back up your claims?

▸ If you have done some work experience in environmental health, can you explain what you learned from it?

▸ Be aware of some current issues or difficulties facing environmental health officers. Is there one that you could talk about in more depth?

▸ Try to identify anything in the subjects you have studied so far that relates to environmental health. Be prepared to expand on this.

▸ Think about the qualities you would need to be a good environmental health officer. Try to give examples.

▸ European Studies

See sample interview questions under: **'Languages'**, **'Geography'** *and* **'English'**.

▸ Film, Radio and TV Studies

See sample interview questions under: **'Media and Communication Studies'**.

▸ Finance

See sample questions under: **'Accountancy'**, **'Business Studies'** *and* **'Economics'**.

▶ Geography, Geology and Environmental Science/Land Economy

Geography

Essential A levels: Most degrees require Geography.

Useful A levels (possibly): Some BSc degrees prefer one of: Biology, Chemistry, Maths or Physics.

Geology/Earth sciences

Essential A levels: Usually two from: Maths, Physics, Chemistry and Biology.

Useful A levels (possibly): Geography and Geology.

Environmental science/studies

Essential A levels: Many courses will ask for two from: Biology, Chemistry, Maths, Physics and Geography or Geology.

Chance of being interviewed: Most courses will make offers on the basis of the UCAS Apply but a significant minority of courses do still interview.

What you need to know

▶ Be prepared to talk in detail about field visits you have been on.

▶ Make sure you are as aware as possible about your own locality. Show that you have taken in as much as possible of the world around you. Also have an awareness of world issues.

▶ Expect questions on the parts of the A level geography syllabus that you have covered.

▶ Mention any magazines that you have read or TV programmes that you have watched, but then be prepared to answer some in-depth questions on these.

▶ These courses contain many practical elements – they are about doing not just thinking. So try to think of examples where you have actually done and completed something, rather than just thought about it.

▶ You may be given a map/photograph/graph/specimen of rock or indeed any relevant object to reflect upon and discuss.

▶ Visit: **www.rgs.org**, **www.geolsoc.org.uk** and **www.ies-uk.org.uk**

Sample interview questions

▶ What geography did you see on your way here?

▶ Where did your interest in geography stem from?

▶ What is the definition of geography?

▶ Why study geography? What do you like about it?

▶ Talk about the geography of a country you know.

▶ In what areas do you think sociology and geography overlap?

▶ What books or articles about geography have you read lately?

▶ What interests you in the field of geology?

▶ Why Land Economy?

- What do you see as the future of Geology?
- What do you want to do with your degree?
- Why are you interested in earth sciences?

- Look at these photographs. What landforms do they show and what types of rocks form these features?
- Tell us what you know about plant succession on dunes.
- What would the world be like without wind?
- What is special about London as opposed to other cities in England?
- What do you think will be the geographical legacy of the Olympics in London?
- What are the environmental problems in the area that you live?

- What did you learn on your geography field trip?
- From the graph showing forty years of carbon dioxide emissions what can you conclude?
- What are the main geographic and economic factors of climate change?
- How can you apply the statistics you have learned on your geography A level course?

- What are the arguments for 'trade not aid'?
- Why may a geographer be well placed to assess the effect of global recession?

- What can be done about issues of land reform in Zimbabwe? (Black vs. white people arguing over land ownership rights.)
- What can the government suggest to increase happiness in local communities without using public spending?
- Why do governments care about CO_2 emissions? Do they do enough in terms of adopting environmentally friendly methods of energy generation?

- Should the government build on green belt land?

Students' comments

- *Interviewer drew a collisional plate boundary and asked me what I knew about it – basic A level knowledge. Then more in-depth questioning: how would you date rocks on mountain tops using Uranium rate of decay. What are the problems with method?*

- *'Know your subject well. Know current events. Know the reasons why you want to study geography.'*
- *'I was asked a lot of questions relating to geography theory, which I was unprepared for as the letter did not indicate that the interview would be formal.'*
- *'He asked me: "Do you have any questions?" So I asked: "How can the position of plate boundaries on the crust change?" This happened to be his area of research and so took up the whole interview!'*
- *'There were 150 people in total and we were split into 13 groups. The group interview was with 3 to 4 people for an hour.'*
- *'I was given 2 graphs showing unemployment and job loss. I was asked to describe patterns and suggest which country's figures were being shown.'*
- *'I was shown a range of maps, data, pictures to analyse and was also given a 5 page document to summarise and identify key, and contentious, issues (lasted 1 hour).'*

▶ History

Essential A levels: Most degrees require History.

Useful A levels (possibly): Economics, English Literature, Philosophy, Politics, Sociology and Theology/Religious Studies.

Chance of being interviewed: Most courses will make offers on the basis of the UCAS Apply, but a significant minority of courses will interview.

What you need to know

▶ You will need to put across your passion for History – with evidence to support this.

▶ Show that you are genuinely interested in periods of History other than those you are studying for your A level.

▶ Think about the links between History and the other subjects you may be studying (for example, English Literature).

▶ Questions will mostly be based on your A level History syllabus, wider reading that you have mentioned in your personal statement and, in a few instances, work that you have sent in or sources that you have been given at interview.

▶ Try to think of examples where you have learned independently and not just relied on your teachers.

▶ Visit: **www.history.org.uk**

Sample interview questions

▶ Why is history important?

▶ Is history really relevant to the present? Even ancient history?

▶ Can we teach objectivity in history?

▶ What do you think people learn from the past?

▶ Why do you want to study history and not science, when the world is crying out for more scientists?

▶ What are the differences and similarities between the sciences and history?

▶ What important history books have you read?

▶ What area of history are you most interested in?

▶ What has been your favourite topic in the history you have studied?

▶ How much does history influence literature or vice versa?

▶ How can artists help historians?

▶ How can historians find out about social history?

▶ How do the citizens of a country influence its foreign policy?

▶ Did Cromwell use his religious beliefs to mask his personal ambition? Why did he execute the King?

▶ For a history essay you have written, what books did you read on the topic? How did the opinions of the various authors differ?

▶ How important is the role of the individual in history? Is it dangerous to attach too much importance to individuals?

▸ In your study of social history, what group of people do you think has been hidden from history? What sources of evidence can we gain from this group?

▸ What is the importance of using first-hand evidence and documents in studying history?

▸ How can we tell whether historical documents are reliable? Even if they are one-sided, are they still useful?

▸ What do you think are your personal biases when you study history?

▸ What do you think of 'women's history'?

▸ Do you think historical novels are useful for historians?

▸ How is a totalitarian regime able to rise to power?

▸ Do you think the Holocaust should only be interpreted by Jewish historians?

▸ Why are current affairs important?

▸ Free trade or fair trade?

▸ Name a situation in current affairs in which views have changed over the past fifteen years.

▸ Define globalisation.

▸ What do you think of proportional representation?

▸ What modern trends are the political parties in Britain setting?

▸ What are the similarities and differences between journalistic and scholarly history?

▸ What career do you want to follow after studying history?

▸ How does your work experience relate to history?

▸ Three words; choose an odd one out. There is no wrong answer: 'educated', 'population', 'electorate'. Argue your case. Then, argue the case of another one.

▸ Why is Jared Diamond's book *Guns, Germs and Steel* useful to historians? (from personal statement)

▸ How useful is biology to historians?

▸ What is a healthy democracy? (from submitted written work)

▸ What are the benefits and limitations of an oral source?

▸ Given two sources thirty minutes before interview – one history, one politics

▸ Various questions on the sources given:

▸ How can historians deal with 'presentism'?

▸ Can political leadership affect the views of the electorate?

▸ How do voter trends affect the ideological beliefs of parties?

Students' comments

▸ *'The interview was generally a discussion about history and he really let me choose the period that I wanted to talk about.'*

▸ *'I had sent in an essay on Mussolini, and particularly about his use of propaganda. The interview was a detailed discussion of the ideas in my essay and how they fitted into the syllabus.'*

▸ *'Many of the questions about the relevance of studying history were repeated many times in different ways – so know your arguments.'*

▸ *'My interview was more of an oral examination on the history A level syllabus. I was not expecting this and had not begun to learn my syllabus in the depth required.'*

▸ *'I was given some sources to look at relating to an issue I knew nothing about. I was then asked questions on these sources.'*

> *'Second interview based on source given 20 minutes previously. Asked to date source, discuss themes from source. Also short discussion on personal statement – given choice of topics taken from this.'*

> *'Invited to pick a topic for second half of History interview to discuss.'*

> *'General discussion about books and lectures mentioned in personal statement. Questions I had on a source were given half hour before interview – specifically about the author's views.'*

▶ History of Art

Essential A levels: None.

Useful A levels (possibly): Art, English Literature, History, Theology/Religious Studies, French, German, Spanish and Italian.

Chance of being interviewed: Most courses will make you an offer on the basis of what is in UCAS Apply but a significant minority of courses do still interview. Be prepared to analyse pictures of paintings or an object.

What you need to know

▶ If you have not studied History of Art before, make sure you have visited galleries and museums. You will be expected to talk about the works of art you have seen and what you felt about them.

▶ Questions will mostly be based on the content of your personal statement.

▶ You may be presented with an image, such as a painting, and asked specific questions about it.

▶ Visit: **www.artchive.com** and **www.aah.org.uk**

Sample interview questions

▶ Why do you want to study History of Art?
▶ Are you familiar with the main European schools of painting?
▶ Who are your favourite artists?
▶ What is your favourite period of art?

▶ Analyse the eight paintings in front of you.
▶ Look at this reproduction of a Rembrandt painting and then talk about it.

▶ What is the difference between studying history of art and history of design?
▶ What do you perceive the history of design to be?

▶ Do you think there is a difference if you look at a subject directly or as a snapshot?
▶ Would you agree that your vision somewhat restricts your ability to look at several things at once which in a way is what a camera does?

Students' comments

▶ *'The first interview really revolved around my personal interests, and how do these relate to art history; then I was presented with a set of images (1950s and 1970s advertisements mainly) and was asked to comment on each and subsequently compare them, perhaps defining some form of connection between the two. The second interview was more based on a discussion on specific artworks. With relation to these pieces of art I was asked about more general notions which surfaced.'*

▸ *'I was given several paintings to analyse. This took up most of the interview.'*

▸ Hospitality Management

What you need to know

▸ These courses provided the basis for careers in hospitality, including jobs such as: hotel manager, restaurant manager, professional chef and receptionist. Find out more by visiting the websites of People 1st (**www.people1st.co.uk**) and the Institute of Hospitality (**www.instituteofhospitality.org**).

▸ Most courses provide training in hotel and restaurant operations, as well as teaching subjects that are very close in content to a business studies degree (but with a hospitality slant).

▸ Relevant work experience is important.

▸ *See sample interview questions under:* **'Business studies'***.*

▸ Information Management

What you need to know

▸ The information management specialist has to deal with a range of sources far beyond books and other printed material. To find out more, visit the website of CILIP, the Chartered Institute of Library and Information Professionals: **www.cilip.org.uk**. CILIP was formed in 2002 following the unification of the Institute of Information Scientists and the Library Association.

▸ *See sample interview questions under:* **'Computer courses'** *and* **'Media and Communication Studies'***.*

▸ International Relations

See sample interview questions under: **'History'**, **'Politics'**, **'Economics'**, *and* **'Geography'***.*

▸ Journalism

See sample interview questions under: **'Media and Communication Studies'***.*

Essential A Levels: None

Useful A Levels (possibly): Any A levels that teach grammar (e.g. Languages). Media related courses may help establish your interest but are not asked for.

Chance of being interviewed: Expect to be interviewed by many of your choices.

What you need to know

▸ Ensure that the course is accredited by at least one of the three industry training bodies – the National Council for the Training of Journalists (print)(NCTJ), the Periodicals Training Council (PTC) and the Broadcast Journalism Training Council (radio, TV and online)(BJTC).

▸ You need evidence of a commitment to this area of work – more important than work experience (that is, however, useful in giving you a taste of the working environment) is evidence of doing things under your own initiative – sixth form newsletter, contributing to an unofficial football website, making podcasts, etc.

▸ Some courses may set you an assignment or task at the interview, usually to check your writing skills.

▸ Visit: **www.bjtc.org.uk** and **www.ppa.co.uk** (Periodicals Training Council), **www.nctj.com**

Sample interview questions

▸ Who is your favourite broadcast journalist?

▸ Here are three stories. Which one would you lead with and why?

▸ Is there a future for newspaper journalism when we can access information in so many different ways?

▸ You have to describe a football match in less than 100 words. What do you think are the essential bits of information that you must include?

▸ Land Economy

See sample questions under **'Geography'**, **'Economics'** **'Surveying'** *and* **'Law'**.

▸ Languages

See also **'Economics'**, **'English'** *and* **'Geography'**.

European studies
Essential A levels: A modern European foreign language, for example, French, German, Spanish or Italian.

French
Essential A levels: French.
Useful A levels (possibly): Another modern foreign language.

German
Essential A levels: German.
Useful A levels (possibly): Another modern foreign language.

Italian
Essential A levels: Italian or another language such as French, German or Spanish. Latin also useful.

Spanish
Essential A levels: Spanish (some degrees will also consider French, German or Italian).

Increasingly, students are choosing to study non-European languages e.g. Mandarin and Arabic. These can usually be started from scratch but you are likely to have to demonstrate a talent for languages.

Chance of being interviewed: Many courses will make offers on the basis of the UCAS Apply, but you should presume that you will get some interviews.

What you need to know

▸ Be prepared for some sort of grammar, comprehension, reading or translation test at the interview. You may be asked to write and/or discuss.

▸ Expect questions on the A level work that you have done, visits abroad and the literature, history, politics, geography and culture of the country that you are interested in.

▸ Read newspapers, magazines and websites in the appropriate language.

▸ Often more than one tutor will interview if you are applying to study more than one language.

▸ Visit: **www.languageswork.org.uk** and the website of the Chartered Institute of Linguists (**www.iol.org.uk**).

Sample interview questions

Many of these questions will apply to any language.

▸ Why do you want to study your chosen language as opposed to any other?
▸ Do you think that language and literature are completely separate and should be studied separately?
▸ Are you better at language or literature?
▸ Which would you like to focus on most at university – literature or linguistics?

▸ Do you think being half French and wanting to do a degree in French is a cop-out?
▸ What are the advantages and disadvantages of translating?
▸ Can translation ever be an art in its own right? When? Give two circumstances.
▸ What do you expect it will be like to learn Spanish from scratch?
▸ How does your study of maths and economics relate to your language studies?
▸ [To a candidate applying to learn Italian from scratch] Look at this poem in Italian with a translation in English. Identify the meaning of each Italian word. Now look at these very different translations of the same poem and compare them.

▸ Is there an element of literature in your French and German A level courses?
▸ Have you studied literature at all? What types of literature interest you?
▸ Do you feel that you will be at a disadvantage doing a literature-based degree when you are not studying any literature-based A levels?
▸ What books have you studied in French? Which ones did you *not* like and why?
▸ Have you read any French books apart from the ones on your A level syllabus?
▸ Look at this poem by Baudelaire for fifteen minutes and then discuss it in the interview.
▸ Look at this passage in French. Is it a poem or drama? What is it about the language that makes you say it is poetic?
▸ What French poetry have you read?

- Have you ever been to Spain? What do you know about Spain?
- What attracts you to Spanish culture?
- Have you read any Spanish literature in translation?
- How has Spain contributed to the arts and humanities?
- What do you know about Spanish architecture?
- Why would Spanish be important in a career/in business/in Europe?
- What books have you read by a Spanish-speaking author?

- What makes an English person English?
- Why is communication important in the EU?
- What do you think of a two-speed Europe and further EU integration?
- Do you think German reunification was a good thing?
- What aspect of European affairs are you particularly interested in?

- Eskimos have fifty words for snow. Russians have no word for privacy. Does this mean they don't have privacy?
- Should prisoners be entitled to privacy?
- Should immigration be allowed?

- The following questions were asked and answered in the relevant foreign language.
- Have you ever been to France? What were your impressions? What shocked you?
- Pretend you are a guide and take me on a tour of the French town where you stayed.
- What are the differences between the French and the English?
- What tensions exist between the French and the English?
- What are the differences between French and English newspapers?
- Define 'existentialism'. Do you believe in it?
- What are the social issues in Paris?
- What do you think of the National Front in France?
- What problems are linked with Algerian immigration to France?
- Tell us about the French political scene.
- Have you been to Germany? Tell us about your visit.
- Do you prefer French or German food?
- What are you studying for your history A level?
- What do you intend to do in your year off?

- (Unseen poem in English.) Tell us something about the poem, linguistic or thematic.
- What is it about?
- What do you make of the title?
- Can the word 'lark' mean anything else besides the definition used in the poem? (General discussion about poem's features)

- (Thirty minutes prep. time for unseen poem in French.) Read the first six sentences of the poem out loud.
- Tell us what you thought.
- Why did it confuse you?
- What is ambiguous?
- What does the phrase 'the lace of the tower' make you think of?
- Talk about the line…
- Do you know an idiom that uses the word 'creux' in French?

▸ How does Chaucer's Middle English compare to the Old French of *La Chanson de Roland*? (that the candidate had read).

▸ Which language did you find easier to understand and why?

▸ Did you notice the French influence on Middle English?

These questions relate to reading the candidate had done:

▸ Which is your favourite poem from Beaudelaire's *Les Fleurs du Mal*?

▸ What did you particularly like about *Le Poison*?

▸ Is it fair for you to say that Beaudelaire writes romantically?

▸ How would you respond to the view that *Les Fleurs du Mal* are religious poems in a sense?

Students' comments

▸ *'The interview was conducted partly in German, partly in French and of course in English. The more intellectually demanding questions were in the main asked in English.'*

▸ *'I was asked to translate a passage of French prose and comment on it. In my Spanish interview I spoke about my interest in foreign films which we then discussed in detail.'*

▸ *'Although the course is not wholly based on literature, I got the impression that it is a very important part. Even in my general interview I was asked to read a poem in English and discuss it.'*

▸ *'The grammar test took one hour and I was given a text in English which I had to answer three questions about and translate part of. No dictionaries were allowed.'*

▸ *'I was asked some difficult questions in French about the passage they gave me to look at, which was very wordy. I was asked a lot about my further reading of French books, but all the literature and personal questions were in English.'*

▸ *'The woman from the Italian department asked me a few questions about the reasons I wanted to study Italian, and asked me if I spoke any. The fact that I couldn't speak any Italian was not a problem at all.'*

▸ *'I was very surprised that I was only asked one question in French, and that we spoke for about twenty minutes about the books I am reading for my English A level.'*

▸ *'We ended with a few questions in French and I had to explain (in poor French, I feel) why I started a French debating society and whether the French are actually hypochondriacs, an issue that I said we had debated.'*

▸ *'I had to do a written test. The first part was a text in English about British and American poetry, which I had to summarise in English. The second part was a text in French, summarised with words missing. I had to find words to fill in the gaps.'*

▸ *'I had to read a short passage and discuss it in Italian. I was then asked questions in Italian about one of the books I had been studying.'*

▶ Law

Essential A levels: None.

Useful A/AS levels (possibly): Critical Thinking (while this will help with the LNAT test, some universities treat it as an excluded subject, and therefore you should always do it as a fifth AS level).

Chance of being interviewed: Most courses will make offers on the basis of the UCAS Apply, although a small number of courses do still interview.

What you need to know

▶ You must be interested in studying law as an intellectual discipline, not just as a means to becoming a solicitor or barrister.

▶ Many questions will be based on what you have put in your personal statement.

▶ It is important, however, to read the law sections in the broadsheet newspapers and follow legal arguments in the press.

▶ Visit some law courts.

▶ *Learning the Law* by Glanville Williams.

▶ *Understanding the Law* by Geoffrey Rivlin.

▶ *Letters to a Law Student* by Nick McBride.

▶ *The Rule of Law* by Tom Bingham.

▶ *Law: A Very Short Introduction* by Raymond Wacks.

▶ *What about Law,* by Virgo et al.

▶ Visit the websites of the General Council of the Bar of England and Wales (**www.barcouncil.org.uk**) and the Law Society (**www.lawsociety.org.uk**).

▶ If you will be taking the LNAT test, prepare yourself by finding out about critical thinking techniques: **www.lnat.ac.uk**

▶ Visit Skills for Justice: **www.skillsforjustice.com**

Sample interview questions

▶ Why do you want to study law? What in particular interests you in the law?

▶ Do you want to be a judge?

▶ What is the point of studying law as an intellectual discipline, as opposed to, say, literature?

▶ How is law more important than politics or economics?

▶ How does a historian's interpretation of law differ from a lawyer's?

▶ Did you choose your A levels with the aim of studying law?

▶ Why do you want to study a whole new subject rather than just carrying on with one of your A level subjects?

▶ How has visiting courts and parliament helped you understand anything you've read in law books?

▶ What law books have you read?

▶ Have you ever visited a court? What did you think?

▶ You don't seem to have any relevant work experience. Why is that?

▸ What recent legal cases have you heard of?

▸ Comment on a current legal issue/case that interests you.

▸ What do you know about the American legal system? What problems does it have?

▸ What are the differences between the US and UK Constitutions and which is more effective from a legal perspective?

▸ Give me an example of how the law could manifest itself in this room.

▸ What would you do to reform the legal system?

▸ What changes would you introduce to the British Constitution?

▸ What are your views on proportional representation?

▸ What do you think about employment law in relation to the sacking of pregnant women?

▸ What is civil disobedience? Do you know any examples of it?

▸ How would any loss of British sovereignty to Europe affect the judiciary?

▸ Do you disagree with capital punishment? Why?

▸ What do you think about censorship?

▸ How do you feel about the lack of women in the higher ranks of the law?

▸ Why do we need laws for acts such as murder?

▸ What is the difference between intention and motive?

▸ What are the advantages and disadvantages of the right to silence?

▸ Define racial hatred. Distinguish between racial, religious, ethnic and political hatred. Is one worse than any other?

▸ How right is it to stop a crime before it has been committed?

▸ Is it ever justifiable to break a promise?

▸ Judiciary vs. legislature – who should make decisions?

▸ Are there any cases when laws should be broken (for example, to defeat Nazism)?

▸ Should Nazi war criminals be tried for their crimes?

▸ Should the law intervene in moral issues? What is the link between law and morals?

▸ Should the state interfere in family matters?

▸ How are the law and politics linked?

▸ What is the Marxist view of law? Does it still apply today?

▸ Are you interested in current affairs? Tell us about a recent news story.

▸ Tell us about a current economic issue.

▸ What books do you read? Tell us about, for example, George Orwell's *Nineteen Eighty-four* and *The Prince* by Machiavelli.

▸ Why is the ECHR important?

▸ Define a white lie and give me an example.

▸ Extract given:

▸ What is this case about?

▸ What opinions were reached by the majority?

▸ What opinions were reached by the dissenter(s)?

▸ What would be your opinion if…?

Students' comments

▸ *'I was given a Cambridge Law Test following interview. I had to choose 1 from 3 essay topics. The test lasted 1 hour. Topics were:*
  – "How should a legal contract be designed?"

- *"Should the jury system be expanded so that juries can decide sentences as well as verdicts?"*

- *"'A' is in his house. 'A' notices a window cleaner ('B') cleaning his windows. 'A' has not met 'B' previously or asked for his windows to be cleaned. 'B' asks for payment and 'A' refuses because he had not asked for the service. Should 'A' pay? Would it make a difference if 'A' had not known about the service?"'*

▶ *'Use 10-15 minutes to plan and structure points. Structure is key. Go with your opinions.'*

▶ *'I was given a discussion sheet with a definition of the offence of battery on it, followed by three different situations. I had to decide whether battery had been committed in each of the situations, according to the given definition.'*

▶ *'I was given a sheet with some statutes printed on it and I was asked to read one of them (which happened to be about theft). I was then given a particular situation to respond to, which was: "Is taking someone's car road-tax disc and returning it after it has expired classified as theft?"'*

▶ *'I had to read a long passage (a side of typed A4 paper) and then say what was illogical about it.'*

▶ *'The legal questions forced me to think on the spot, and we discussed issues in what seemed to me to be great depth. He was interested not so much in my answers, but my reasoning.'*

▶ *'I was a given a definition for a new law on a white board and asked to discuss and develop a better definition.'*

▶ *'The questioning was designed for me to respond, though at times I felt it was too aggressive. Having said that, for a law interview it seemed fair as they were able to judge my arguing skills and the way I responded to rigorous questioning.'*

▶ *'Many of the questions posed could be interpreted in a number of ways and there was plenty of opportunity to guide the conversation to talk about the areas of law that I knew about.'*

▶ *'In the second interview I was given a statute on a criminal act about destroying property and I was given legal problems and asked if the defendant could be prosecuted based on that statute. Then we had a debate about whether the police should keep hold of prisoners' DNA after they've been released.'*

▶ *'We were given a legal extract (a court case) and then given 30 minutes to read it. We were then asked questions on the case.'*

▶ *'Two interviews: In the first, I was given 60 minutes to read a judgement which was then discussed. In the second interview (half based on pre-reading material). Questions were based on principles changing to meet different examples.'*

▶ *'Advice: Read "What about Law", Virgo et al (Virgo was the interviewer for Downing where I had my interview!). Follow news – read law sections (Guardian and Times) and "Comments" sections.'*

▶ *'At times, interviewer appeared to snigger at remark made. Hold your own and do not react under pressure/be intimidated.'*

▶ *'Both interviews based on scenarios:*
  - *First interview – I was given a definition of a charity. Decide whether scenario equates to a charity.*
  - *Second interview – given fictitious law regarding squatting. Scenario was given and I was asked to apply the law with the facts changing all the time. This was followed by discussion over state regulation of cars and the role of EU.'*

▶ *'Questions based on extract given before interview. I was asked which side of case he agreed with and why.*

– Extract given 40 minutes before interview in room with 3 others. 10 minutes reading time and 30 minutes annotation time. Questions were based on the case: What is the argument of claimant? What is the argument of defendant? What was held in the original hearing (extract from appeal case). Then given alternative scenario and asked how previous arguments (of which side agreed with), would apply in this scenario.

– Advice: look for ways in which the original case/judgement can be distinguished from the new scenario provided, thereby proving that your argument still holds. However, if argued into a corner and interviewer proves your argument is no longer valid, concede!'

▸ Leisure and Recreation Management

See sample interview questions under: **'Business Studies'** and **'Sports Studies'**.

▸ Linguistics

See sample interview questions under: **'Languages'**.

What you need to know

▸ Linguistics is the scientific study of languages in general – that is, how languages work and how people use language. It can cover subjects such as: how languages developed historically; phonology (the study of sounds); grammar (as it applies to all languages); meaning; the sociological aspects of language such as dialects and accents; and the biological aspects of how our brains acquire language.

▸ Interviewers will mostly be concerned with why you want to do the course and what steps you have taken to find out about it.

Sample interview questions

▸ What do you understand by the term 'linguistics'?
▸ Name some sounds in English that foreigners get wrong.
▸ Talk about some grammatical structures that differ between English and another language you know.

▸ Marketing

See sample interview questions under: **'Business Studies'**.

▶ Materials Science

(Including Biomedical Materials Science)

See sample interview questions under: '*Biology*', '*Chemistry*', '*Engineering*', '*Natural Sciences*' *and* '*Physics*'.

▶ Mathematics

Essential A levels: Maths and sometimes Further Maths.

Useful A levels (possibly): Physics and Philosophy.

Chance of being interviewed: You should definitely expect to be called for some interviews.

What you need to know

▶ The interview will be about *maths*! Any questions about your social life or outside interests will only be included to put you at your ease. At some Oxbridge colleges you may have more than one interview.

▶ As well as your strength in maths, you need to be enthusiastic. Show proof of your love of maths – for example, through wider reading, entering competitions and/or joining maths clubs.

▶ One book worth reading before your interview is *How to Solve It* by Pólya.

▶ Visit: **www.ima.org.uk**

Sample interview questions

▶ Which are your favourite topics in maths?
▶ How do you think science is portrayed in the media?
▶ What career are you interested in after your degree?
▶ Define the concept of differentiation from first principles.
▶ Give examples of situations where differentiation is *not* possible.
▶ How would you show that integration is the opposite of differentiation?
▶ How would you explain integration and differentiation to a sixth-former?
▶ Differentiate x^2 and $\sin x$ from first principles.
▶ Integrate $\int x (nx)\, dx$.
▶ Draw graphs of $x^2+y^2=1$ and $x^3+y^3=1$.
▶ Draw graphs of $y=\sin x$ and $y=\sin(x^2)$.
▶ Prove that $\sqrt2$ or $\sqrt3$ is irrational.
▶ How does one find 2 to the power of $\sqrt2$?
▶ Prove that every fourth value of the Fibonacci series is a multiple of 3 and that every third value is even.
▶ Let $z=1+2i$. Show in an Argand diagram z, $3z$, iz, $/z/$ and $\sqrt z$.
▶ Prove that in any function that maps from (0 to 1) to (0 to 1) there is at least one fixed point.

▶ Factorise the difference of two squares x^2-1
▶ Substitute into the above $(x+a)^2-b^2$

- Prove that $1+10$ cannot be a square number.
- Sketch the curve $y = \dfrac{2x^2 + 13x - 8}{x^2 - 7}$
- Explain the Product Rule for differentiation from first principles.

- Find 0.9999 to 3 decimal places.
- Prove that n3-n is divisible by 6.
- Sketch $y = \dfrac{\cos x}{x + \pi/2}$
- Sketch $y = \dfrac{x}{\sin x}$ for $0 \le x \le 2\pi$.

- From 1-100, how many multiples of 2; 3; 2 or 3; 2 or 3 or 5?
- Graph sketched and asked to calculate velocity.
- Prove that if you write a positive integer in every square of an infinite grid such that number ≤ mean of 4 neighbours, all numbers must be the same.
- What about if your car used negative numbers, too?

- From 1-100, how many multiples of 2; 3; 2 or 3; 2 or 3 or 5?
- 51 numbers from 1–100. Will there always be 2 that add up to give 101?

- $\int(ax + b(1-x)) = x \int(a) + (1-x) \int(b)$ Describe graph.
- Find symmetries of a tetrahedron – worked through with interviewer.
- Sind all sets of numbers, s, for which if x s and y s, then (x-y) s.

- Sketch $y = e^{1/x}$.
- Show that $1 + \frac{1}{2} + 1/3 + \frac{1}{4} + 1/5 + \ldots$ gets arbitrarily large.
- a<b<c;   a + b + c = 6;   ab + bc + ac = 9;   Prove that a<1<b<3<c<4.

Students' comments

- (Oxbridge) *'No reference to personal statement. I was given a set of questions to answer. I was asked to choose 1 to discuss, plus supplementary question to work through in relation to this chosen question. I expected 2 interviews and was given a third.'*
- *'The interview was very friendly and informal and when I was stuck with problems the interviewers were ready to prompt me.'*
- *'The interview included a whole load of questions on differential equations. I also had to do a test for which calculators were not allowed (despite not being told this beforehand).'*
- *'The interview was more a case of us working together on how to show integration as the opposite of differentiation. He didn't expect me to know how to do it, but he wanted to see how I could think my way through it and solve it with his help.'*
- *'He said he was pleased to speak to someone who could have a conversation as opposed to just sitting down in silence. Reading* New Scientist *that morning proved to be a good idea!'*
- *'You should practise sketching questions that have developmental parts. For example, sketch (1) y=sin x, (2) y=sin2 x, (3) y=sin2x2.'*
- *'1 hour, multiple choice test evening before interview. At the beginning of formal interview I was given a chance to say where thought mistakes were made – I was given my paper back to point out specifics.'*
- *'Given 6 questions the evening before first interview and asked to do at least 2. Two other interviews at different Colleges (Oxbridge selection).'*

▶ Media and Communication Studies

*See sample interview questions under: '**Journalism**'.*

Essential A levels: A few courses specify English or Media Studies.

Useful A levels (possibly): English, Media Studies, Sociology and Psychology.

Chance of being interviewed: While many courses will make you an offer on the basis of your UCAS Apply, a significant minority of courses still interview.

What you need to know

▶ You need to be very clear about the sort of media course you are applying for. Some are more theoretical, others more practical. If yours is one of the more practical courses, do you know exactly what it will train you to do? Also, these courses by themselves will not normally guarantee you a job in the media. So, do your reasons for applying *correspond with* the content of the course?

▶ Many media courses will expect to see some sort of work experience or examples of taking initiative (for example, writing a sixth-form newsletter or contributing to a website).

▶ Try to think of examples (with evidence) of occasions when you have worked in a team. This is very important in media industries.

▶ Some courses may set you an extra test or assignment at the interview, usually to check your writing skills and spelling.

▶ Skillset is the Sector Skills Council for creative media covering: TV, film, radio, publishing, interactive media, computer games, photo imaging and facilities: **www.creativeskillset.org**

Sample interview questions

▶ How did you hear about the course?
▶ What do you consider to be the strengths and weaknesses of working in a team?
▶ What is your favourite aspect of film making e.g. camera work or editing, and why? (from personal statement)
▶ What other institutions have you applied to?

▶ Define the word 'media'.
▶ Have you done any research into the media?
▶ Do you have any interests or hobbies that would be of benefit to a course in journalism?
▶ What are you hoping to do in the future?
▶ There are more people on media courses than there are jobs at the BBC. Why do you think you are going to get into this industry?
▶ How do you think your sociology A level will help you with this course?

▶ What impact do you think digital technology is having on the broadcasting industries?
▶ What is your favourite TV programme and why?
▶ Should the government renew the BBC's charter?
▶ How important is the *Today* programme on Radio 4?
▶ What is the difference between online and offline editing?
▶ What newspapers do you read? Talk about an article you read yesterday.

▸ Who is your favourite broadcast journalist?

▸ Have you recorded yourself speaking? In what way do you think your broadcast voice can be improved?

▸ Presuming that you have read a newspaper on the way to the interview, what story interested you most and why?

▸ Think of somebody who has a dreadful public image. How could we improve their reputation?

▸ Explain the formula for 'mission documentaries'.

Students' comments

▸ *'The interview day for my course in broadcast journalism involved a current affairs test and a group interview. The current affairs test was quite simple, but you do have to be well informed about recent news stories and past and present media magnates. I made a silly mistake from not being aware of the names of certain important media people! However, I think much of the selection process was based on how you presented yourself in the group interview. You have to be yourself and be clear.'*

▸ *'I was expecting to be asked about my work experience. Most of the interview consisted of questions relating to media issues I had covered in sociology A level.'*

▸ *'I was asked to take along anything creative.'*

▸ *'I had a group interview lasting 2 hours. The discussion covered: changes in TV over time, including with the arrival of the Internet, and the future of TV.'*

▸ *'Questions were based on visual portfolio and show reel taken.'*

▸ *'Be prepared for reflective questions on your portfolio and show reel i.e. what you think you did well, what you could have done differently, etc.'*

▸ Medicine

See separate chapter

▸ Microbiology

See sample interview questions under: **'Biology'**.

▸ Music

Essential A levels: For most courses, Music A level plus Grade VII or VIII.

Chance of being interviewed: You should presume that you will be interviewed for all your choices and at interview you could be tested on one or many of the following areas (look at the prospectuses for the individual entry requirements for each course).

Performance	Aural
Keyboard	Harmony and counterpoint
Sight-singing	Extracts for analysis or 'naming of composer and period'

What you need to know

▸ Make sure that you are clear about the type of course you are applying for and why you want to do it. While there are still a large number of traditional courses, there has been a growth in popular and commercial music courses. Even among traditional courses, some put more emphasis on musicology while others emphasise performance.

▸ If you are very interested in performance, make sure that you can explain why you do not want to go to a *conservatoire*.

▸ You should expect questions to be based on the interests you have expressed in your personal statement. If you have mentioned a composer, expect questions on his or her use of instruments, harmony, counterpoint, time signatures and other compositional techniques, as well as historical setting, influences and so on.

▸ You need to have a wide grounding in music history – do not just rely on what you have studied for your music A level. As well as your areas of particular interest, you must have an overview of the Renaissance (1400–1600), Baroque (1600–1750), Classical (1750–1800), Romantic (1800–1900) and Modern (1900 onwards) periods.

▸ Visit the Incorporated Society of Musicians (**www.ism.org**) and the British Recorded Music Industry (**www.bpi.co.uk**).

▸ Creative & Cultural Skills is the Sector Skills Council for advertising, crafts, cultural heritage, design, music, performing, literary and visual arts: **www.ccskills.org.uk**

▸ Conservatoires Admissions Scheme: **www.cukas.ac.uk**

Sample interview questions

▸ Why here?
▸ Do you know what you want to do after university?
▸ Do you enjoy performing?
▸ What sort of music do you like?
▸ Do you enjoy all types of music?
▸ What was the last concert you went to?
▸ Is there a performer you particularly admire?
▸ Have you written any original compositions? Describe them for us.
▸ Who has influenced your own compositions?
▸ What impact do you think digital technology is having on music?
▸ What is the role of live performance?
▸ How can you make a living in music?
▸ Do you think sequencing software is taking the skill out of music?

▸ Do you think Bach is an important composer?
▸ What do you learn from harmonising in the style of Bach?
▸ What do you know about madrigals?
▸ Explain Haydn's influence on chamber music.
▸ How did Beethoven help develop the symphony?
▸ In the romantic period, what political and social changes affected composers?
▸ In what way did Debussy challenge the musical language of his time?
▸ What influenced Stravinsky?
▸ Why were patrons important?

All questions based on a performance piece:

▸ Do you think this piece has a clear structure?
▸ Is there a particular recurring motif?
▸ Aside from resonance, how did the use of the electric guitar help to bring out the piece?

▸ What particular aspect of our course interests you?

Students' comments

▸ *'The most important part is your performance. I was asked to perform some Grade VIII flute music and I was also required to do some sight-reading and aural tests.'*

▸ *'It was much simpler than I had been prepared for with my mock interview. The actual performance of the candidate is the top priority with most musicians, rather than any knowledge of musical history.'*

▸ *'I was asked what the exam board was for my grade 8 exam. A range of questions stemmed from that E.g. which pieces, what periods etc.'*

▸ *'I was given a written task, a choice of 2 pieces to play and a score on which I had to comment in terms of style, history, mood, musical/technical features.'*

▸ *'Audition, done first – given 10 mins to warm up. Asked to prepare 1 or 2 pieces lasting no more than 5 minutes.'*

▸ *'Written test – Given a choice of 2 pieces (both played twice), given a score for both – asked to choose one to comment on the use of compositional technique to evoke emotion.'*

▸ *'Asked to do a harmony exercise during interview. Asked to bring in a composition, a piece of harmony work and an essay (from A level course).'*

NB: These comments would not hold true for certain courses, for example at Oxford or Cambridge.

▸ Natural Sciences

See also sample interview questions under: 'Biology', 'Chemistry', 'Maths' and 'Physics'.
Essential A levels: Normally three out of Biology, Chemistry, Maths and Physics.

What you need to know

▸ While this course is well known as a Cambridge course, similar courses exist at a number of other universities as well. Most of the sample interview questions come from Cambridge.

▸ The course can really suit talented scientists who are not yet sure which direction they would like to take. It can also suit those who know what they would like to specialise in the future, but who want to cover more general science areas first.

Sample interview questions

▸ What aspects of science are you interested in and why?
▸ Describe an article you have read recently in the *New Scientist* and discuss it.
▸ What is the last book you read?

- How aware should the public be about scientific developments?
- Which three science subjects would you choose for your first year Natural Sciences course?
- What have you been doing in Chemistry?
- Describe your last chemistry practical.

- What is the volume of a water molecule? Calculate, not estimate.
- When cycling, what area of rubber on a bike tyre touches the ground?
- Draw a graph of a solid being heated.
- Why is it worse to be scalded by gas at 100°C than water at 100°C?
- Explain Newton's second law of motion, defining the terms you use.
- Describe and explain what is happening to a ruler balanced on one end when it falls on: a) smooth surfaces; b) rough surfaces. Why does the base slip?
- How would a body behave if it was removed from the plane of an ellipse of a solar system?
- Why do high tides occur twice in twenty-four hours?
- Why does an egg spin when it is hard boiled?
- How can waves travel through a vacuum?
- How does light behave as both a wave and a particle?

- What is gravity?
- What is the equation for simple harmonic motion that includes gravity?
- Why does a bar magnet fall slower through a metal tube than a wooden one?
- Prove that in a game of pool, after a white ball collides with a red ball that is at rest, the velocities of the two balls are very nearly perpendicular.
- Is it possible to see an object through adjacent faces of a glass cube? (the refractive index of a glass is 1.5)
- A bouncy ball is dropped h metres from rest into a rigid wooden board inclined at 45° to the horizontal. Assuming no energy is lost in the collision, prove that the ball rebounds horizontally and find the distance it first bounces to the point it next bounces.
- Two identical pendulums are in different rooms. The only difference is that there is a large block of lead covering the floor in one of the rooms. What would be the difference between the oscillations of the two pendulums?

- How does an X-ray interact with a crystal?
- How would you increase the efficiency of a bar heater with a fixed voltage across it?
- How does a mass spectrometer work?
- How does infrared spectroscopy work?

- Draw the differentiate $y = \sin x - x$.
- Draw $y = 1/1 - x^2$.
- Why does a magnet slow down when falling through a copper tube?
- Explain the photoelectric effect.
- A train of mass m carries four carriages of mass m. What is the tension between each carriage?
- What speed would a ball need to be travelling at so as not to fall towards the centre of a bowl, with radius r? The ball has mass m.
- Mechanics questions about a rubber; forces acting on it and a graph of its movement if it had a constant vertical force and a constant horizontal velocity.
- Plot $y = A(e^{k-1})^2$. (Given 20 minutes.)

- Will a primary, secondary or tertiary halogenoalkane react fastest with OH- in a non-polar solvent? (partly from personal statement).
- Will adding a CN- group opposite the OH in phenol increase or decrease pKa? Why?

▸ Questions about groups (e.g. NO_2) bonding to phenol and the relative changes in pKa that they would cause.
▸ Describe the NMR spectrum of ethanol.
▸ Why do you get a 1:3:3:1 ratio from the CH_3 group?
▸ What is the importance of photochemical reactions? How do they occur and how do they lead to the photoelectric effect?

▸ What interests you about genetics?
▸ Talk about DNA and describe protein synthesis.
▸ What is a chromosome and what is it made of?
▸ How do we end up with 46 chromosomes in each cell after cell division if every cell normally has 46 chromosomes?
▸ How does meiosis create genetic variation – two ways?
▸ What is the human genome project and why is it useful?
▸ If you are religious, do you have a problem with Darwin's theory of evolution? What other theories of evolution are there?

▸ What type of rock is this [shown rock sample] and how can we date it?
▸ Why is it important to use fossils to date rocks?
▸ What problems are there with the environment?
▸ Talk about a scientific discovery that has revolutionised its field.
▸ Work out which is biggest and smallest, without evaluating, the integrals (all between e and 1) of: lnx, $ln(x^2)$ and $ln(x^2)$.
▸ Draw a graph of $y = \frac{1}{4} - x^2$
▸ If I gave you a substance, what tests would you do to tell me what it was?
▸ The speed of computers doubles every one and a half years. Could you write an equation for this?
▸ Without integrating, rank in order of size: lnxdx; lnx^2dx; $(lnx)^2dx$.
▸ What is the difference in bonding that results in the difference in the nature of liquids (especially water), solids and gases?

▸ Describe what you can see [shown a monkey's brain in a jar].
▸ Compare the brain of a mouse with that of a human.
▸ Plan an experiment to show that a mouse does not have colour vision.
▸ Why do you think that the human brain has so many folds in the cortex?
▸ How is a rat less complex than a human?
▸ Why would a rat not need colour vision?
▸ Describe what you can see [shown a tube of dirt, debris and seeds]. How would you test for any living organism in this tube?
▸ What does this look like to you [shown a video clip of a small, moving insect]. What do you think it is doing?
▸ What is the function of the nucleolus?
▸ Describe how viruses replicate.
▸ Why does the flu virus change each year?
▸ What affects the mutation rate of a virus?
▸ How would you inject nerve cells to replace those in the brain? (from personal statement)
▸ Calculate the total number of amino acids that can be made.
▸ Tell me about the Biochemistry taster course you attended. (from personal statement)
▸ Draw a molecule of ethane – estimate its bond length.
▸ You are given a freezer, measuring cylinder and balance. How could you use these to help estimate bond length?

▸ How would you measure/calculate the volume of molecule of ethane?

▸ As organism size increases, what part of an organism would be most affected if simple diffusion occurred?

▸ What is the mechanism of ventilation?

▸ What is the difference between inspiration and expiration when you exercise?

▸ Compare aerobic to anaerobic respiration.

▸ How do we typically define a mammal?

▸ How could we test that organisms are from the same species?

Students' comments

▸ *'I was asked academic questions on chemistry (addition polymerisation, esterification), physics (metal stresses, simple harmonic motion) and maths (integration, polar coordinates). The interviewers deliberately chose topics that I said I hadn't covered in my A level studies. They are more interested in how you think and respond to new situations, than in how much you know. All you can do as preparation is brush up on your A level work to act as a foundation for the unfamiliar situations you will be presented with.'*

▸ *'Whenever I told them that I hadn't yet covered certain topics at school they said, "Good, let's talk about it."'*

▸ *'The interview opened with a question about what interested me in the subject and I mentioned an article I had read. He then asked me questions about this for nearly the whole interview. If I had realised, I would have mentioned a topic that I really knew about, rather than something I found fascinating but didn't know much about.'*

▸ *'I was given thirty minutes to look over some unseen reading before the first interview. I then had to the sit a Thinking Skills Assessment (TSA) which was much harder than the practice TSA provided online. I would recommend taking critical thinking A level.'*

▸ *'All questions were factual despite interviewers stating that they were interested in thought process rather than factual answer.'*

▸ Nursing and Midwifery

*See sample interview questions under: '**Professions allied to Medicine**'.*

▸ Nutrition

*See sample interview questions under: '**Professions allied to Medicine**' (Dietetics) and '**Biology**'.*

▸ Occupational Therapy

*See sample interview questions under: '**Professions allied to Medicine**'.*

▸ Optometry (Ophthalmic Optics)

Essential A levels: Two from Biology, Chemistry, Maths or Physics (some courses prefer Biology as one of the choices).

Chance of being interviewed: You should expect some interviews.

What you need to know

▸ You will need to explain fully why you want be become an optometrist and provide evidence to back up your claims.

▸ If you have done some work experience in optometry, you will be asked to explain what you learned from this time.

▸ It is a good idea to be aware of some current issues or difficulties facing optometrists. Is there one that you could talk about in more depth?

▸ Think about what qualities you would need to be a good optometrist. Try to think of examples.

▸ Visit: **www.college-optometrists.org**

Sample interview questions

▸ Why do you want to study optometry?

▸ Where did your interest in optometry come from?

▸ What did you learn from work shadowing?

▸ When you were on your work experience, what eye defects did the optometrist have to deal with?

Students' comments

▸ *'I wasn't really asked anything about optometry. The interviewer seemed more interested in the personal section of my UCAS Apply.'*

▸ *'The first question she asked was, "Why optometry?" You must be clear on this.'*

▸ Pharmacology

*See sample interview questions under: **'Biology'**, **'Chemistry'** and **'Pharmacy'**.*

What you need to know

▸ Cogent is the Sector Skills Council for the chemicals and pharmaceuticals, oil and gas, petroleum and polymer industries. Visit: **www.cogent-ssc.com** and **www.bps.ac.uk**

▶ Pharmacy

See sample interview questions under: **'Biochemistry', 'Chemistry'** *and* **'Natural Sciences'**.

Essential A levels: Taking Chemistry and two from Biology, Maths and Physics will keep the vast majority of courses open to you. Some courses specify Chemistry, Biology and Maths. Taking Chemistry and Biology keeps most courses open.

Chance of being interviewed: You should expect to be interviewed by most of your choices.

What you need to know

▶   You will be asked to explain fully why you want be become a pharmacist and provide evidence to back up your claims.

▶   If you have done some work experience in pharmacy, you will need to be able to explain what you learned from this time.

▶   It is a good idea to be aware of some current issues or difficulties facing pharmacists. Is there one that you could talk about in more depth?

▶   Try to identify anything that you have studied so far that relates to pharmacy. Be prepared to expand on this.

▶   Think about what qualities you need to be a good pharmacist. Try to think of examples.

▶   Visit the website of the Royal Pharmaceutical Society of Great Britain: **www.rpharms.com**

Sample interview questions

▶   Why do you want to study pharmacy? Why not medicine?
▶   Have you had any practical experience of working in pharmacy?
▶   What do you think medical pharmacy involves?
▶   What other areas of pharmacy are there (for example, in industry)? What do you think they involve?
▶   What do you think is the role of the pharmacist?
▶   How did you find out about pharmacy? Have you done any research into careers in pharmacy?
▶   What career do you want to go into?

▶   Talk about a topic you are currently learning in biology or chemistry.
▶   How do you make a one-molar solution of sodium chloride?
▶   What does the liver do?
▶   What is an ECG (electrocardiogram)?
▶   What is the difference between a drug and a medicine?

▶ Philosophy

Essential A levels: None.

Useful A levels (possibly): Maths, Classical Civilisation, Philosophy and Religious Studies/Theology.

Chance of being interviewed: Most courses will make offers on the basis of the UCAS Apply, but a significant minority of courses do still interview. Some law questions are also relevant here.

What you need to know

▸ A good starting point is to read *Philosophy: The Basics* by Nigel Warburton. Then try Bertrand Russell's *Problems of Philosophy*.

▸ You may be asked to sit a test or write an essay at the interview.

▸ Visit: **www.royalinstitutephilosophy.org**

Sample interview questions

▸ Why do you want to study philosophy?

▸ Have you read any books about philosophy?

▸ What interests you most about philosophy?

▸ Alice is driving a car. Sees neighbour she dislikes. Intentionally swerves and kills neighbour. Bob is driving a car. Has mechanical fault and swerves into neighbour and kills him. Should they both receive the same amount of blame?

▸ Charles is drunk. Decides to drive home. Loses control of car, mounts pavement and kills pedestrian. Debbie is drunk. Decides to drive home. Loses control of car, mounts pavement, but no-one is there to be injured. Should they both receive the same amount of blame?

▸ Ernst was brought up in pre-war Germany. Rises through Nazi ranks to become head of concentration camp killing thousands of Jews. Franz lives in Argentina, having moved there pre-war. Grown up in multicultural society and is tolerant and accepting of all. Had Franz grown up in Germany, he would have followed same fate as Ernst. Discuss.

▸ 'All sea creatures swim. Everything that can swim can fly, therefore all fish can fly.' Is this valid?

▸ 'Everything has a course. If everything has a course, I am not free. I am free.' Which sentences agree with one another and which sentence(s) do you agree with?

▸ X has a ship. After every month he replaces one plank with a new one. After ten years no original plank remains. Y has taken every original plank and remade the ship exactly as it was. Which of the ships are numerically one and the same as the one X owned in the beginning?

▸ Which of these three sentences are the most similar? All bats are blind. All mothers have babies. All water is made up of hydrogen and oxygen.

▸ If most lawyers are rich and most rich people live in the countryside and most country people go fishing on Sundays, does it follow that most lawyers go fishing on Sundays?

▸ If you keep adding grains of sand, one at a time, when does it become a heap? If you take away grains of sand one at a time, when does it stop being a heap? Is this a valuable intellectual debate?

▸ If it takes two to make a fight, when there's an argument are both sides equally to blame?

▸ I have promised my class a surprise exam one week in an eight-week term. Which week can I give it in?

▸ Why do we seek supernatural explanations for the unusual (for example, a tossed coin showing heads 1000 times) but not for the usual (for example, bodies obeying the laws of gravity)?

▸ If cosmic beliefs are religious, are religious beliefs cosmic?

▸ Discuss this statement: 'It has not yet been proven that God doesn't exist.'

▸ Does God exist?

▸ Is time travel possible?

- If your body is scanned and then destroyed and a perfect copy of your body and mind is instantaneously created on Mars and you 'wake up' there remembering everything, are you the same person?
- Is there more to a person than body and mind?
- Is teleporting a type of transport?
- Different societies have different moral standards. Is morality therefore subjective?

- Why is a bag of diamonds more expensive than a glass of water? When might this change?
- What is the difference between Mill's principles of utilitarianism and the rights of an individual?
- Can a business act morally when its aim is to maximise profits?
- Is it the nature of man to be altruistic or to promote his own interests?
- When is it OK to break a law? Who says when a law is unjust?
- How does one balance the views of two different cultures, for example in the case of the *fatwa* against Salman Rushdie?

Students' comments

- 'He assumed I had no prior knowledge of philosophy unless I told him otherwise.'
- 'It was very relaxed and informal and the discussion took the format of giving different arguments for and against several philosophical topics ranging from politics to theology.'
- 'Before the interview I was given a paper with five statements and arguments. I had twenty minutes to pick two to discuss in the interview. For example: "I might be wrong about anything I know. Therefore I might be wrong about everything I know."'
- 'I had to do a written test, stating the differences between words in pairs and then incorporating them in sentences to convey their meanings. The pairs were: accident/mistake; short/succinct; deny/refute; contradict/disprove; uninterested/disinterested.'
- 'He started to bombard me with unanswerable philosophical questions: "Why are we here?"; "What is life if it isn't a dream?" I was thoroughly confused and found it absurd and a little unfair that he expected me to answer such questions with no philosophical background at all, as if I had already done the course.'
- 'I had 25 minutes to look at unseen material – one article on personal identity, several scenarios on the theory of moral assessment. Half the interview was on personal identity, the other half on moral assessment.'
- 'Given a set of rules regarding the validity of an argument. Given a series of arguments and discussed whether they were valid or not. Spoke about free will/cause and effect.'

▸ Photography

What you need to know

- Visit the websites of the Association of Photographers (**www.the-aop.org**) and the British Institute of Professional Photography (**www.bipp.com**).
- Creative Skillset is the Sector Skills Council for creative media covering: TV, film, radio, publishing, interactive media, computer games, photo imaging and facilities: **www.creativeskillset.org**

▸ Look at the sample interview questions under: **'Art and Design'** and **'Media and Communication Studies'**.

▸ Go to exhibitions.

▸ Build up a portfolio of your own works and be prepared to be questioned on it.

Sample interview questions

▸ Who are your favourite photographers?

▸ What is it that inspires you about photography?

▸ Tell us about the area of photography that most interests you.

▸ What do you want to engage with in the medium of photography?

▸ Who inspires you?

▸ Why do you want to study photography?

▸ What particular area of photography interests you most?

▸ Talk us through your portfolio – questions based around portfolio, self-evaluation.

▸ What's in the news at the moment and how are events being covered by photographers?

▸ What books do you read? (other than photographic)

▸ If you were given £60,000 what would you do with it?

▸ Who are your main influences?

▸ In-depth questioning on favourite photographer.

▸ Questions on specific photographs from portfolio – why they were taken, what student was trying to say.

▸ Is there anything else you would like to say to support your application?

Students' comments

▸ *'Portfolio was looked at, but not discussed.'*

▸ *'Asked to take essay on particular photographer, or their work.'*

▸ *'General discussion on portfolio and photography in general – not all specific.'*

▸ Physics

See sample interview questions under: **'Natural Sciences'**, **'Chemistry'** *and* **'Engineering'**.

Essential A levels: Maths and Physics.

Useful A levels (possibly): Further Maths and Chemistry.

Chance of being interviewed: Most courses will make offers on the basis of what is in UCAS Apply, but a significant minority of courses do still interview.

What you need to know

▸ Interview questions will tend to relate to what you have already studied at A level (including mechanics and pure maths), as well as subjects you have mentioned on your personal statement.

- Sometimes there may be a test at the interview. This could be written or the questions could be asked orally.
- Look at relevant questions under 'Natural Sciences'.
- Visit the website of the Institute of Physics: **www.iop.org**

Sample interview questions

- What area of physics interests you most? Would you like to specialise in this area?
- Tell me about a current Physics topic.
- What do you like about Particle Physics?
- Tell me about any practical skills that you have learned outside of the school course.

- Give an example of your problem solving abilities.
- What are the four basic forces in physics?
- What is the equation for simple harmonic motion?
- If there is a capacitor in the middle of two coils with an electron beam shot through the middle of the capacitor, why is the beam deflected when a current runs through the coils?

- If a centripetal force is acting inwards, why do you feel thrown outwards when travelling around a bend in a car?
- If an anchor is thrown out of a boat into a lake, will the water level of the lake rise or fall?
- Are the molecules in a solid stationary?
- If you displaced a molecule in a solid and then let go, would it go back to its original position?
- Why do light spectra radiate from the centre of the surface of a compact disc?
- Being in space is associated with weightlessness. What does weightlessness mean to you?
- Galileo timed light and heavy objects rolling down inclined planes. How do you think he timed the rolling?
- Would you expect all records to be broken were the Olympic Games to be held in a hall on the moon?
- A sheet of white paper is viewed through a piece of blue glass and the paper looks blue. Why?
- What do you know about the ways in which atoms are arranged in a solid? What happens when the atoms in a solid are heated?

- What is the relationship between the number of molecules of gas per unit volume and the number that hit area A, with velocity v in time t?
- Give me an equation relating energy and distance.
- Differentiate $v^2 e^{-av}$.
- Work out the equation for the power of a wind turbine and how wind speed affects it.
- Estimate the time taken for a jumbo jet to fly from London to Sydney.
- How are flame tests analogous to nuclear decay? (from personal statement)
- What would be observed during a flame test under high pressure? (From personal statement).
- What would you do to a radioactive sample to cause it to decay?
- Sketch the graph of $y = A/x12 - B/x6$.
- Why doesn't tea taste as nice at high altitudes?
- How does pressure change with height?
- How many atoms are there in the sun?
- Why do we see a rainbow?
- Why is a rainbow one big arc and not lots of tiny rainbows?
- If you have a car travelling at 10ms-1, attached to an elastic band that is attached to a post, and there is an ant crawling on the elastic band towards the car, will it ever reach the car?

- Why do planes not make very sharp turns?
- What is the smallest radius a plane can turn through without the pilot blacking out?

For astrophysics:

- Tell us what you know about the origins and evolution of the universe.
- What is the Hubble constant?
- Does the earth turn clockwise or anticlockwise?
- What is the equation explaining a star's orbit in its galaxy?
- Explain why it is suggested that dark matter is what keeps stars in orbit at a constant relational velocity even as they are found further from the centre of a galaxy.
- How are the Northern Lights formed?

Students' comments

- *'A thinking skills assessment (TSA) was taken on the day of interview.'*
- *'I was also asked some maths questions about integration and something else to do with complex numbers that we hadn't covered at school yet.'*
- *'Questions were asked on everything we have done for A level so far. The questions were occasionally badly worded making it difficult to understand what was wanted.'*
- *'The interviewers were happy to give help if they saw you were in trouble and did not just leave you to baffle over the questions.'*
- *'Had been given offer prior to interview. This was an opportunity to ask detailed questions about the course.'*

▸ Physiology

See also **'Biology'** *and* **'Chemistry'**.

Essential A levels: Chemistry and Biology would keep most courses open.

Useful A levels (possibly): Maths and Physics.

Chance of being interviewed: Most courses will make you an offer on the basis of what is in UCAS Apply but a significant minority of courses do still interview.

What you need to know

See sample interview questions under: **'Biology'** *and* **'Medicine'**.

Visit: **www.physoc.org**

Sample interview questions

- Why did you apply specifically for physiology?
- Why not medicine?
- What are you looking to gain from the course and the university?
- What medical/biological stories have you read in the news recently?
- What do you think about animal testing?

- How would you argue against someone saying testing drugs on rats can have little or no benefit to a human because they are different creatures?
- Can pain in animals be justified? To what extent can pain be inflicted for the benefit of human research?
- How does a neurone act? How does it work?
- What is the importance of a myelin sheath? What would happen if it was removed?
- How can a DNA mutation occur?
- What is the shape of a synapse?
- Name some neurotransmitters.
- What neurodegenerative disorders do you know of? Tell me about one.
- Do you know what causes schizophrenia or multiple sclerosis?
- MS is caused by the degradation of the myelin sheath. Suggest causes for this.
- MS is genetically inherited. Why doesn't everyone with the MS gene contract MS?
- Why doesn't MS affect someone from birth if it is in their genes?
- What is the immune system?
- What environmental factors could affect whether or not someone gets MS?
- Why could viruses affect whether the person gets MS or not?
- What is the difference between a pump and a channel?
- Describe the reabsorption mechanism of the kidney.
- If two parents are homozygous recessive for albinism, how can they have a child who is not an albino?
- If neither parent is an albino, how can they have a child that is?
- What is the main disease in the UK that needs to be researched compared to that in the world as a whole?

Students' comments

- *'I was given 25 minutes to write an essay on "Plumbers save more lives than doctors. Discuss".'*
- *'I was asked a really complicated question on blood pressures, given different tubes and asked to draw many graphs!'*

▶ Physiotherapy

*See sample interview questions under: '**Professions allied to Medicine**'.*

▶ Podiatry

*See sample interview questions under: '**Professions allied to Medicine**'.*

▸ Politics

Joint degrees and other courses involving Politics are included under the relevant subjects.
See sample interview questions under: 'History' and 'Economics'.

Essential A levels: None.

Useful A levels: Politics, Economics, History, Philosophy, Sociology and Law.

Chance of being interviewed: Most courses will make you an offer on the basis of what is in UCAS Apply, but a significant minority of courses do still interview.

What you need to know

▸ If you are not taking Politics A level, you should still have done some reading around political philosophies, political history and the workings of government.

▸ You need to be aware of the political world around you by following current affairs.

▸ Try to find out more about the politics of a country other than the UK.

▸ Questions at interview will tend to be based on your current studies and what you have put in your personal statement.

▸ Visit: **www.psa.ac.uk**

Sample interview questions

▸ Why are you interested in politics?
▸ What political ideology are you most attracted to?
▸ How active are you in politics and what are your views?
▸ Who would you vote for in a general election and why?
▸ Tell us what you think about the current political situation in Britain.

▸ Does your vote count?
▸ Is Britain a democracy? How could it be made more democratic?
▸ What are your views on electoral reform?
▸ What system of proportional representation should Britain introduce?
▸ What do you think about reform of the House of Lords?
▸ Does Britain need a bill of rights?
▸ Discuss the differences between the views and policies of the Labour, Conservative and Liberal Democrat Parties.
▸ What would you do if you were prime minister?

▸ Is the EU a Federal System?
▸ Why were there riots in London in 2011? What caused them? [Given four pictures for reference.]
▸ How much power do MPs really have?
▸ If you were commissioned by the UN to write a report on how globalisation affects human happiness, how would you go about it?
▸ What do you think about Europe and the European Union?
▸ Does Britain have control of its monetary policy when it is part of the European Union?
▸ What do you think about the euro?
▸ If there were a more federal Europe, what control would Britain have over its own policy?

- Does the media provide impartial reporting?
- Is there, or should there be, censorship of the media?
- Do the owners of newspapers determine their content?
- How aware do you think the general British public is about politics?
- Is there a correlation between the number of political parties, the voting system and ethnic groups?

- What are the differences between the political systems of the United States and the United Kingdom?
- What do you know about American politics?
- Are the US Primaries democratic?
- Are you surprised about the Presidential result?
- How would you define a developing country?
- Why do you think some countries are developed and others underdeveloped?
- Why should we give aid to other countries?
- In what ways was the conflict in Northern Ireland similar to the current situation in the Middle East?
- What do you think about Zimbabwe?
- Tell me about the French political system. [This was after having been given relevant reading material for twenty minutes].
- Is it legitimate for a country to intervene in another country's affairs? Why?
- Is it legitimate if it's an organisation like NATO?

- Define ideology.
- Is environmentalism an ideology?
- Tell us about Marxism.
- What is the main principle of liberalism?
- What is the difference between power and authority?
- Distinguish between: right and good; just and fair; nation and state.
- What role does economics play in politics?
- What should the role of the church be in politics?
- Comment on this statement: 'It is inevitable that there will be conflict between state and freedom.'
- Do you think we are freer with laws?

- What period of history are you most interested in? What have you learned from it?
- Map out the history of Russia, up to the present day, for someone who knows nothing at all about it.
- What are you reading?
- Name a book that has had an effect on your view of politics or economics.
- Comment on the way some European nation states have retained their monarchies. What have you read related to this?
- Do you perceive Barack Obama to be black, white, Kenyan, American?
- Why do you think the working-class majorities did not rise up against the Liberals in the 1800s and redistribute wealth?

- Discuss the merits of democracy
  [Given a sheet about where a political party would be on the political spectrum. Given a number of other political parties in the system and asked to mark where they would be on the spectrum.]

Students' comments

▸ *'The interviewer asked very general political questions, such as "Is Marxism dead?" and let me lead on to subjects I felt strong in.'*

▸ *'They didn't ask any particularly interesting questions but they did persist on every point I made and forced me to really develop every answer.'*

▸ *'The interview would have been a lot harder had I not done politics A level.'*

▸ *'Before the interview we had to read a passage about the merits and demerits of the welfare state, and two tables of results from the French elections in 1958 and 1962. I had to answer questions on these in the interview, for example saying what the election results indicated. It was tricky stuff and I felt I kept getting things wrong.'*

▸ *'It was very personal. I was asked who I would vote for in a general election, and who my parents vote for and why.'*

▸ Professions allied to Medicine

Dietetics
Essential A levels: Chemistry and Biology.

Nursing and Midwifery
Essential A levels: Some courses ask for Biology or another science.

Occupational therapy
Essential A levels: Some courses ask for Biology. Some will also consider Psychology, Physical Education, Sociology or another science.

Paramedic Science
Essential A levels: Some courses ask for a science such as Biology. Some will also consider Physical Education, Psychology or Sociology. Also category C1 on your driving licence (vehicles weighing between 3,500 kg to 7,500 kg)

Physiotherapy
Essential A levels: Most courses will consider you with just Biology. However, some ask for a second science from Chemistry, Maths or Physics.

Podiatry
Essential A levels: Courses normally require at least one science, and usually prefer Biology. Some courses specify Biology plus another science.

Radiography
Essential A levels: Most courses ask for one science A level, a few ask for two.

Speech and language therapy
Essential A levels: Some courses require a science such as Biology, Chemistry or Physics (some specify Biology). However, some will consider candidates with none of these.

Useful A levels: A modern foreign language (French, German, Spanish or Italian), English Language (and Literature) and Psychology.

Chance of being interviewed: You should expect to be interviewed and prepare for this.

What you need to know

▶ **Dietetics**: The dietician's skill is to translate the science of nutrition into understandable and practical information about food and health. Contact the website of the British Dietetic Association (**www.bda.uk.com**).

▶ **Nursing and midwifery**: These courses train you to become a hospital or community nurse, health visitor or midwife. Contact NHS Careers (**www.nhscareers.nhs.uk**), the Royal College of Nursing (**www.rcn.org.uk**) and the Royal College of Midwives (**www.rcm.org.uk**).

▶ **Occupational Therapy**: This can also be called rehabilitation therapy. It is concerned with helping people with physical and mental disorders to live a full life by overcoming as much as possible the effects of their disability. Contact the British Association of Occupational Therapists and College of Occupational Therapy (**www.cot.co.uk**).

▶ **Paramedic Science**: A Paramedic is the senior ambulance service health care professional at an accident or a medical emergency. Working on their own or with an emergency care assistant, they assess the patient's condition and then give essential treatment (**www.collegeofparamedics.co.uk**).

▶ **Physiotherapy**: Physiotherapists use exercises and movement, electrotherapy, manipulation and massage to treat the injured, disabled, sick and convalescents of all ages for a large variety of conditions. Contact the Chartered Society of Physiotherapy (**www.csp.org.uk**).

▶ **Podiatry**: The Society of Chiropodists and Podiatrists can be found at **www.scpod.org**

▶ **Radiography**: Diagnostic Radiographers use X-rays, ultrasound and magnetic resonance imaging (MRI) to produce images of the body. Therapeutic Radiographers are involved in the treatment of cancer. Contact the Society of Radiographers (**www.sor.org**).

▶ **Speech Therapy**: Speech and Language Therapists assess and treat all kinds of voice, speech, language and swallowing problems. Contact the Royal College of Speech & Language Therapists (**www.rcslt.org**).

▶ For all the above career areas: **www.nhscareers.nhs.uk**

▶ You will need to be able to explain fully why you want to enter your chosen career and provide evidence to back up your claims.

▶ If you have done some work experience that relates to this career, you will be expected to explain what you learned from it.

▶ It is a good idea to be aware of some current issues or difficulties associated with this career. Is there one that you could talk about in more depth?

▶ Think about what qualities you would need for this career. Try to think of examples.

▶ You may well have tests for numeracy and literacy.

Sample interview questions

▶ How will you manage your time – work/social/volunteering?
▶ What do you think will be your greatest challenge at university?
▶ What makes you different?

▶ What are the differences between working as a dietician in a hospital and in the school meals service?
▶ What issues face dieticians?
▶ What topics have you studied for your Chemistry A level that relate to nutrition?

- Why do you want to do midwifery?
- When have you faced conflict and how did you deal with it?
- What is the role of a midwife?
- Have people been negative about you choosing midwifery?
- What is the difference between a community and hospital midwife?
- How would you manage working shifts/nights?
- What are your views on home births?
- What coping strategies do you think you need if a patient has a stillbirth?
- What role do you see for the partner in the birth process?
- What do you feel antenatal education should involve?
- Do you think mothers make better midwives?
- How does a midwife differ from a nurse?
- Tell me about some of the current issues facing midwifery.

- What do you see as the role of a nurse?
- Why do you want to do nursing?
- Why do you particularly want to do children's nursing?
- What qualities do you have that would make you a good nurse?
- In what ways would you help a stroke victim?
- If a colleague was doing something wrong, what would you do?
- What could get in the way of a team in a hospital working together?
- What does 'care' mean to you?
- With your A levels in science you could have done other health careers, why nursing?

- Why do you want to become an occupational therapist?
- On your work experience did you see the occupational therapists working with other professionals? How did they do this?
- What do you think occupational therapy involves?

- Why do you want to be a paramedic?
- What qualities do you think make you suitable?
- What qualities do you think you will learn?
- Do you have a C1 on your driving licence? [necessary for ambulance driving]
- What clinical intervention can a paramedic provide?
- What can a paramedic do to protect an airway?
- What reading have you done?
- What career progression do you think you will have as a paramedic?
- Name an issue affecting paramedics. What do paramedics need to do? What does the NHS trust need to do?

- How did you choose physiotherapy?
- Why do you want to be a physiotherapist? How did you get involved in physiotherapy and how long have you been interested in it?
- What qualities do you think a physiotherapist needs? Do you have them?
- What does physiotherapy involve?
- What areas do physiotherapists work in?
- What steps did you take to find out more about physiotherapy before you applied?
- What did you learn from your work experience?
- Are your A levels relevant to physiotherapy?
- What do physics and maths have to do with physiotherapy?
- How would you deal with a difficult patient?

- Do you play sport?
- How can you manage sport and study?

- Which types of patient do podiatrists come into contact with?
- What did you learn from your time at a podiatry clinic?

- Which other professionals would use a radiography department?
- What is the difference between diagnostic and therapeutic radiography?

- Why do you want to do speech therapy?
- What sparked your interest in such a specialised area?
- What qualities does a speech therapist need? Do you have them?
- Tell us about your work placement. What did you learn from it? Did it reaffirm your decision to do speech therapy?
- What have you learned from speech therapy clinics you have visited?
- Have your A levels taught you anything that would be relevant to speech therapy?
- Have you read any books about speech therapy?
- What do the terms 'linguistics', 'phonetics' and 'neurological impulses' mean to you?
- How does phonetics work?
- Do you think there are medical and teaching elements in a speech therapist's work?
- What are the problems with speech therapy?
- Why might parents not take their child to speech therapy sessions?
- Do you think deaf people should be encouraged to use sign language or learn verbal skills?
- Courses in this area have various names – speech therapy, speech science, speech pathology. Are there differences? What do you know about this particular course?

Students' comments

- *'I had a group interview with 7 candidates. We discussed how government policies on nursing could be improved. We were scored on "knowledge", speaking, body language, communication, listening and teamwork.'*
- *'I had a written comprehension test plus a non-calculator Maths test before the interview.'*
- *'We watched a video (about one-and-a-half minutes long) about a man who had suffered a stroke and the effect it had had on his speech. Then we had to discuss it in the interview.'*
- *'We had to take part in a one-hour activity about delayed auditory feedback, which we had to answer questions on afterwards.'*
- *'As part of my physiotherapy interview they asked to see my hands, to check for any problems.'*
- *'My first physiotherapy interview included a physical examination, which was not a problem. However, while I was getting dressed I was being asked several questions at the same time so, between ripping my tights and putting my jumper on, my answers were slightly muffled!'*
- *'Prepare for basic clinical questions.'*
- *'I had a 40 minute numeracy and literacy comprehension test.'*
- *'I was given literature about the course/university beforehand – read for preparation! Also get a provisional C1 on your driving licence. You have to be 18 to take the test.'*
- *'There were 3 group sessions before a 1:1 interview. The complete process took a full day.*
    - *Mind map on role of a paramedic / what should be taught on the course*
    - *Problem-solving scenario*
    - *Designing a flag! (be prepared for anything!)'*

▸ *'For my midwifery group interview – first I was asked 2 questions individually and then a group discussion:*
  – *Please tell me about 1 or 2 experiences that made you want to become a midwife*
  – *Please talk me through a relationship/event that you have encountered that you found difficult to deal with. What did you do? What did you learn from it?*
  – *There was also a discussion on why women do not receive the quality of care they should.'*

▸ *'There was no formal individual interview. There were group activities in groups of four.*
  – *Write down points relating to 4 areas of midwifery: skills, influences, knowledge, experiences*
  – *Individually asked to say something positive about the group idea*
  – *There was also a Maths test – good GCSE level.'*

▸ Psychology

Essential A levels: A few courses ask for one of Biology, Chemistry, Maths or Physics.

Useful A levels (possible): Biology, Maths, Psychology and Sociology.

Chance of being interviewed: Only a small number of courses interview applicants.

What you need to know

▸ If you want to become a professional Psychologist, make sure the course has been accredited by the British Psychological Society.

▸ Psychology degree courses do not involve helping people with their problems! You will be studying subjects such as personality types, defining and testing intelligence, perception, memory and developmental psychology.

▸ The main reasons for rejection are a lack of reading about psychology and not understanding what is involved in a Psychology degree course.

▸ It is helpful to know the differences between the different branches of psychology: clinical psychology, educational psychology, occupational psychology, criminal and legal psychology.

▸ Visit the website of the British Psychological Society (**www.bps.org.uk**).

Sample interview questions

▸ Why do you want to study psychology?
▸ What aspects of psychology are you particularly interested in?
▸ Are humans the most intelligent species?
▸ Why do you want to do a BSc in experimental psychology rather than a BA in psychology?
▸ Why do you particularly want to do social psychology?
▸ What do you want to do after your psychology degree?

▸ What books have you read about psychology?
▸ What have you learned about psychology through your other A level subjects?
▸ What do you think you will be studying in the first year of your psychology course?

▸ How could you determine whether people with autism feel any emotional response seeing as you can't gauge this through language?

▸ Do you know what a psychology experiment is? Have you ever carried one out?

▸ Design a psychology experiment concerning colour blindness.

▸ How could you devise an experiment to find out if animals see in black and white?

▸ What is perception?

▸ What is the benefit to psychologists of a person who has been blind all their life and then regains their sight?

▸ Do you think Milgram's obedience studies could be done again?

Students' comments

▸ *'There was no need to be nervous. You just have to know why you want to do your course and be confident.'*

▸ *'I was given an information sheet and asked to evaluate an experiment: a) the effect of anti-depressants in causing healthy people to remember positive stimuli b) a graph of the effect of the drug on memory using 10 pictures showing people before and after the drug.'*

▸ Quantity Surveying

See sample interview questions under: **'Surveying'** and **'Accountancy'**.

▸ Radiography

See sample interview questions under: **'Professions allied to Medicine'**.

▸ Religious Studies and Theology

Essential A levels: None.

Useful A levels (possibly): Religious Studies/Theology, Philosophy, English Literature and History.

Chance of being interviewed: Most courses will make offers on the basis of what is in UCAS Apply, but a significant minority of courses still interview.

What you need to know

▸ There is no need to be religious to study many of these degrees. In fact, if you are very conservative in your beliefs you may not enjoy the majority of courses in this field.

▸ An attempt to gain some knowledge of a broad range of religions will be welcomed.

▸ Questions in interviews will generally be based on your current studies, information you have put in your personal statement and topical issues.

▸ Visit: www.multifaithcentre.org

Sample interview questions

▸ Why do you want to study theology?

▸ Why do you want to study divinity rather than religious studies?

▸ Do you believe in a God? How can you prove his existence?

▸ What is a miracle?

▸ What do you think about 'Pascal's wager'?

▸ What other religions interest you as well as Christianity? Why?

▸ Do we need religion to understand human existence?

▸ What do you think the influence of Socrates has been?

▸ What do you think is the importance of religious architecture?

▸ What are your views on genetic engineering?

▸ What do you think is the difference between theology and philosophy?

▸ Discuss the perspectives of the Chief Rabbi vs. Richard Dawkins – from personal statement.

▸ Discuss historical vs. metaphorical truths.

Student's comment

▸ *'I was given a pack on Genesis and then had to make a presentation on how relevant Genesis 1 and 2 were for a contemporary theology of creation.'*

▸ Social Policy

See sample interview questions under: **'Politics', 'Sociology', 'History'** *and* **'Economics'**.

▸ Social Work

Essential A levels: None.

Useful A levels (possibly): AGCE/Diploma Health and Social Care, Sociology, Psychology and Law. You must have grade C or above in English and Maths GCSE.

Chances of being interviewed: You should expect to be interviewed and prepare for this.

What you need to know

▸ You will need to show an understanding of social and community work at a basic level. Read *Social Work Practice* by Veronica Coulshed and Joan Orme.

▸ You must have an understanding of, and an ability to define the meaning of, discrimination. What does it mean? How does it manifest itself? How can it be challenged?

▸ You will need to demonstrate a commitment to this career path through work experience (paid or voluntary).

▸ All candidates have to be police checked (but a criminal conviction will not automatically exclude you).

▸ Read *Anti-Discriminatory Practice* by Neil Thompson.

▸ Visit: **www.hpc-uk.org** and **www.skillsforcare.org.uk**

Sample interview questions

▸ What does a social worker do?

▸ Can you talk about some of the issues affecting social work in general?

▸ Think about your voluntary work or work experience. Can you think of two changes you would make that would have improved the service delivered?

▸ What qualities and skills do you think a social worker needs?

▸ What qualities and skills do you think you can bring to social work?

▸ Which of your qualities and skills would you like to develop or improve while you are on the course?

▸ What has been your experience of academic life to date?

▸ Can you talk about an idea or theory that you have studied that has influenced your views?

▸ Can you give an example of discrimination that you have experienced or observed? How was this dealt with?

▸ If you were faced with an unpleasant scenario (for example, having to interview an aggressive parent who has been mistreating their young child) how do you believe you would cope?

▸ What client group would you like to deal with on qualification? Why?

▸ Should disabled students go to mainstream schools?

▸ Sociology

Essential A levels: None.

Useful A levels (possibly): History, Politics, Sociology, Psychology, Geography and Media Studies.

Chance of being interviewed: Most courses will make offers based on the content of the UCAS Apply, although a minority of courses do still interview.

What you need to know

▸ If you are not taking Sociology A level, you should do some introductory reading on the key themes of: social theory; social change; social identities and structures.

▸ Interview questions will tend to be based on your current studies and on issues you have raised in your personal statement.

▸ It is a good idea to keep abreast of current affairs and issues that interest you that affect society, past, present and future.

▸ Visit: **www.britsoc.co.uk**

Sample interview questions

▸ Why do you want to study sociology?

▸ What are you looking for from a course on sociology?

▸ State three social problems that exist in Britain and explain them.

▸ As a sociologist, how would you explain crime?

▸ Why do eighteen-year-olds commit crimes?

▸ Can schools play an important role in reducing criminal behaviour, particularly among eighteen-year-olds?

▸ Are single-parent families a symptom or a cause of instability in society?

▸ What is social policy?

▸ What newspapers do you read? What makes a good columnist?

▸ What books do you read?

▸ If you went to India to do marital relationships research and found that the norm was to marry for practicality, not romance, but then found that the major Bollywood hit at the time was based on romantic relationships what would you make of it?

Students' comments

▸ *'Be topical. Have a listen to the news or read the paper on the day of the interview.'*

▸ *'I mentioned that I was interested in crime and deviance, which I had studied at AS level. This led to a long discussion. If you're going to bring something up, read up on it first.'*

▸ Speech Therapy

See sample interview questions under: **'Professions allied to Medicine'***.*

▸ Sport and Physical Education

Essential A levels: Many courses want to see one of Biology, Chemistry, Maths, or Physics.

Useful A levels (possibly): Physical Education and Psychology.

Chance of being interviewed: Most courses will make offers on the basis of the UCAS Apply but a significant minority of courses do still interview.

What you need to know

▸ You need to be clear about the type of course you are applying for. Sports courses tend to cover physiology, psychology, sports performance, coaching and the business and administration of sport. A leisure management course will be more like a business studies course; a sports journalism course is a journalism course; a sports therapy course is closer to a physiotherapy course.

▸ Interviewers will be very interested in your sporting history to date. Reread your personal statement to make sure you got this across. However, being a talented sportsperson is not enough in itself to get you on to a course.

▸ Visit the websites of Sport England (**www.sportengland.org**) and the Sport and Recreation Alliance: **www.sportandrecreation.org.uk**

▸ SkillsActive is the Sector Skills Council for the active leisure and learning industry embracing sport and fitness, outdoors and adventure, playwork, camping and caravanning: **www.skillsactive.com**

Sample interview questions

▸ How can we get more children involved in sport?
▸ Why do you want to do a degree in sports science?
▸ What is your favourite sport and why?
▸ Why do you think football is much more popular than hockey in the UK?
▸ How do you think you could improve your sporting performance?
▸ Why do you want to train as a PE teacher after this degree?
▸ Do you agree that athletes using banned substances should not be allowed to compete?
▸ If you are so interested in physiology, why haven't you applied for a physiotherapy degree?
▸ What is the best sort of diet for your sport? Why?
▸ Are you considering a career related to sport?
▸ Why do you think the armed forces encourage so much sporting activity?
▸ What do you think is the best way to coach children in your sport?

▸ Statistics

*See sample interview questions under: '**Mathematics**'.*

▸ Surveying

Essential A levels: None.

Useful A levels (possibly): For some types of surveying (for example, building surveying) Maths and Physics could be helpful. For estate management (general practice surveying) most A level combinations will be considered.

Chance of being interviewed: Most courses will make offers on the basis of the UCAS Apply, however a significant minority of courses do still interview.

What you need to know

▸ Surveying is the measurement, management, development and valuation of anything and everything – whether it is natural or man-made.

▸ There are different types of surveying. The main ones are: general practice surveying (valuation, estate agency, auctioneering and property development); quantity surveying (building accountants); building surveying; land surveying; mineral surveying.

▸ For more information, contact the Royal Institute of Chartered Surveyors (**www.rics.org**).

▸ Interviewers will be concerned with why you want to enter this career field and what you have done to find out about it, for example through work experience.

Sample interview questions

▸ Why do you want to do quantity surveying?

▸ Do you know what quantity surveying is?

▸ What do you know about quantity surveying? How did you find out about it?

▸ Why are you interested in a career in property?

▸ Do you know the difference between retail and commercial property?

▸ What is 'buy to let'?

▸ When you did your work experience, what kind of business was the company you went to involved in?

▸ What experience do you have of dealing with customers?

▸ You have done arts A levels. How will you cope with some of the technical parts of the course?

▸ What will you do with your degree?

▸ Tourism

What you need to know

▸ *See sample interview questions under:* '**Business Studies**'. Most of these courses are a business degree with a travel and tourism slant.

▸ Think about any positive or negative experiences you have had whenever you have left your normal environment.

▸ Try to think of any evidence that you can provide about your personal qualities (for example, communication skills).

▸ Visit: **www.uksp.co.uk**

▸ Town and Country Planning

What you need to know

▸ You will need to explain fully why you want to enter this career and provide evidence to back up your claims.

▸ If you have done some work experience that relates to this career, you will be expected to explain what you learned from this time.

▸ It is a good idea to be aware of some current issues or difficulties associated with this career. Is there one that you could talk about in more depth? Perhaps you could visit a new town in the UK.

▸ Think about the qualities you would need for this career. Try to think of examples.

▸ *See sample interview questions under:* '**Geography**', '**Architecture**' *and* '**Surveying**'.

▸ Visit: **www.rtpi.org.uk**

▶ Veterinary Science

Essential A levels: You need to take Chemistry and Biology, plus either Maths or Physics, in order to keep all seven courses open to you.

Chance of being interviewed: You should expect to be interviewed and prepare for this.

What you need to know

▶ You will need to explain fully why you want to become a vet and provide evidence to back up your claims.

▶ It is important to have done some relevant work experience and be able to explain what you learned from it. To play safe, you should have done two weeks in a veterinary practice, two weeks with large domestic animals or livestock and two weeks with other animals (kennels, stables, zoo, etc.).

▶ There is often a focus on your personal qualities and interests.

▶ It is a good idea to be aware of some current issues or difficulties facing vets. Is there one that you could talk about in more depth?

▶ Some vet schools will want you to take the BMAT: **www.bmat.org.uk**

▶ Think about what qualities you would need to be a vet. Try to think of examples.

▶ Visit the website of the Royal College of Veterinary Surgeons (**www.rcvs.org.uk**).

Sample interview questions

▶ Why do you want to come to this university? Why does it stand out from other vet schools?

▶ Why do you want to read veterinary science?

▶ Why are you here today?

▶ What do you think about our course/uni? Have you been to open days, etc.?

▶ Which of the sciences do you prefer? Why?

▶ Which aspect of biology do you enjoy most?

▶ What was your most valuable work experience, and why?

▶ What was your most challenging work experience?

▶ What was your most enjoyable work experience?

▶ This is a very competitive course, why would you make a good vet?

▶ Why is being a vet your desire?

▶ What do you think are the best and worst aspects of being a vet?

▶ What are your weaknesses? How will these affect you as a vet?

▶ What is your weakest subject at the moment? How will you overcome this weakness to get the grades you need?

▶ Veterinary science is a very intense course, what would you do to relax?

▶ What would you like to specialise in if you became a vet?

▶ If you were to focus on a particular aspect of veterinary medicine, and had a year to do it, what would you choose?

- Could there be an NHS for animals?
- What would you do if someone brought in a fat cat? Further questions relating to the rate of obesity rising in pets and horses, and why that is.

- How is it possible for swine flu to be present in humans and pigs? [Follow up questions were on antibodies anti-gens.]
- How can mastitis can be cured/prevented? Why does it arise?
- How much does a spay/castration cost?
- What do you know about fly strike, mastitis and blue tongue? [plus follow up questions.]
- Why should equipment be sterilised before use?

- Should animals have equal rights to humans? Why?
- What is your opinion on keeping animals in zoos?
- In what cases should an animal be put down?
- What is your opinion on animal cloning?
- What is your opinion on intensive rearing of domestic livestock?
- Are you in favour of badger culling? Why?
- Would you treat an animal hit by a car if the owner can't afford to pay?
- Would you rather be a caged rabbit or a wild rabbit?

- What precautions should be taken when avian flu is present?
- How do lambs gain immunity from their mothers? How is this different to humans?
- What do blood tests check for?

- Why are animals still used for medical research when there are other alternatives?
- What advice would you give to someone thinking about owning a pet dog?
- What vaccinations should be given to kittens/puppies?

- Why aren't all pigs vaccinated against swine flu?
- What do you know about farm management? E.g. dairy/sheep.
- Would you prefer to work with small or large animals?

- What do you know about getting work/jobs post graduation?
- Describe a surgical procedure you witnessed.
- What did you learn about the positives/negatives of the career?
- What do you know about plant-based treatments replacing current veterinary drugs?

- What dilemmas do vets face in their profession?
- Talk about the quarantine laws with respect to rabies.
- How do vaccinations work?
- With respect to mammals, are herbivores on the whole larger than carnivores? Why are they larger?
- Horses and cattle have similar digestive systems. What disease do they have in common?
- What are your views on animal experimentation?
- If you felt a pig farmer was being cruel to his livestock, what would you do?
- Are you a vegetarian?
- Could the government handle bovine TB more effectively?

- How are physics and maths applied to veterinary science?
- Describe an experiment you have carried out in one of your science subjects. Explain what happened and why.

- How is penicillin absorbed into the blood?
- Discuss heart pressure in the ventricles and aorta.
- What is the difference between an embryo and a foetus?
- Draw graphs of the drug concentration in blood after oral medication and via injection.
- How would you do a pregnancy test on cows?
- Talk about the cell membrane. Give an example of a substance that protein molecules allow into the cell.
- Where does respiration occur in cells? Explain the theory behind the presence of mitochondria in cells.
- Talk about the differences between gases, liquids and solids, with particular reference to water.

Students' comments

- *'I was given an animal skull to analyse, identify and talk about the teeth.'*
- *'I had to fill in a lengthy questionnaire in advance and I was asked a large number of questions based on this.'*
- *'The process took the whole day. First we had a group challenge for about 10 of us with an examiner (and a video camera filming us), and we were given a number of scenarios and had to put them in order of severity/priority. I then had a practical assessment with some blind testing/touch and had to guess what I was feeling (a cow's tongue!). I then had to do a diabetes test on dog urine and explain the results followed by a maths test related to how an ORH drip works. Finally I had an interview with 2 lecturers.'*
- *'The process began with spending 5 minutes at each of 8 tables, which were:*
  1. *This was a diagram of glucose homeostasis, and I was asked to describe what was happening at each stage*
  2. *Very heavy focus on current diseases. He fired questions at me about TB, blue tongue, orf, swine flu. It was very intense!!*
  3. *Asked about my personal statement, pretty basic stuff like the most interesting case I had seen; a difficult situation I had either been in or seen and how I overcame it etc*
  4. *Had to describe a typical spay/castration operation. They asked me what anaesthetic was, asked the typical hours of a vet, and what I think is the best way to cope with animals dying/suffering. Also asked why I hadn't been to an abattoir.*
  5. *This was a weird ethical scenario where the vet was doing an operation on my neighbour's cat to sort out a stomach ulcer, and I was supposed to be the work experience student watching the operation. Half way through a piece of metal, or something like that, drops into the stomach and the vet searches for it but can't find it so stitches up the cat after sorting out the ulcer and doesn't say anything. A month later my neighbour comes up to me and says their cat died they don't know why. The interviewers asked me what I thought I should do in this situation E.g. Would I tell them what the vet did etc?*
  6. *Another diagram which showed the sudden drop in males taking veterinary science and increase in females. They asked me why I thought that was and how I think this will change plus some other random questions!*
  7. *This was a rest station.*
  8. *Basically questions on why I wanted to come to X university, why I wanted to be a vet and other "standard" questions.'*

▸ 'I was given some scenarios about (i) an old lady with a dog who was her best friend and he's really ill and needs to be put down and she's refusing. They asked me how I would handle this situation (ii) where a vet had basically not given the service he should have as the clinic offers home visits and he couldn't be bothered to go, so didn't and made up some lie. They asked me what I thought should happen to him and what the worst thing was about the situation. I said he should get fired and not be allowed to do vetting until he is retrained and learns the code of conduct, and the worst thing was the animal was left suffering (this was the first time they actually nodded at my answer).'

▸ 'There were a number of ethics issues discussed such as: animal cloning; slaughtering policy; racehorse ethics.'

▸ 'I had to learn some topics in advance: BSE, scrapie, blue tongue, TB, dangerous dog atc, e-coli, foot and mouth, brucellosis, avian flu, mastitis, anthrax.'

▸ "Learn' your personal statement!'

▸ Zoology

See sample interview questions under: **'Biology'** and **'Veterinary science'.**

Index of university subjects

Notes